THE EIGHTH VEIL

ANN TODD

THE EIGHTH VEIL

G. P. Putnam's Sons
New York

Library of Congress Cataloging in Publication Data

Todd, Ann, date.
   The eighth veil.

   1. Todd, Ann, date. 2. Actors—Great
Britain—Biography. I. Title.
PN2598.T39A34   1981   791.43′028′0924 [B]   81-7378
ISBN 0-399-12662-7   AACR2

Printed in the United States of America

With thanks for
their encouragement
Lydia—Nicholas—Claude
Audrey—the Rev. Neil Smith—Jan
Unity

With my love
to
Justinian

CONTENTS

THE EIGHTH VEIL

CHAPTER 1

The Seventh Veil

Though I had been acting on the London stage for some years, it wasn't until the last year of the war that I had my first really big chance in life. Sidney Box, the well-known film producer, came to see my performance in the play *Lottie Dundass* several times; then he and his wife, Muriel (she is now Lady Gardiner), sent me the original script of *The Seventh Veil*. In this story the girl was the only person who appeared on the screen. The other characters were to be filmed in shadow "voices-off" and reflections in the piano and mirrors—avant-garde and experimental for that time. I was much too frightened to try to carry my first important film role by myself, and my husband, Nigel Tangye, and my agents agreed, so Muriel and Sidney changed the script and showed all the other characters on the screen, and gave me a part that seemed especially made for me.

We started filming without a leading man and worked for three weeks while Sidney tried desperately to find one. I was practically unknown in films, especially in America, and no one wished to play with me.

At last Sidney gathered us all together and said that we couldn't go on unless the money was forthcoming and we had a star. I stood rooted to the ground, unable to speak. Sidney, who had given me this great chance and so much encouragement, came over to me and said: "This is when you need courage. Many actors before you have had to take this sort of blow, it is how you take it that matters; let's hope for a miracle." That night I prayed and prayed. I must have worn God out.

At the end of the week we had our miracle. James Mason agreed to play the part. You can't fight destiny. One door closes and another one opens and the pieces begin to fit into place—the jigsaw puzzle of life.

The Seventh Veil has everything—a bit of Pygmalion, a bit of *Cinderella*, a bit of Svengali. Apart from all this, it is an intriguing psychological drama, one of the first films to have a hero who was cruel. Most male stars up to then had been honest, kind, upstanding, good-looking men whom the female star was supposed to feel safe and secure with for the rest of her life when they finally got together at the end of the film. Not so with our smash hit. The men in the audience saw me as a victim, and the females thrilled to Mason's power and cruelty, as women have thrilled to this since the world began, however much they deny it. That is why I think it was such a tremendous success! It is interesting, too, that this film has a lot of sex in it though there are no love scenes between Mason and me; in fact he never touches me all through the film.

The story is about an orphan aged fourteen played by

me and called Francesca. She is sent to live with her guardian, Nicholas (James Mason), a recluse who makes it plain when she arrives that he has no time for her and does not want a female in the house anyway. However, he plays the piano well himself and soon discovers that she has outstanding gifts in this direction. He becomes determined to devote himself to making her into a really great performer. Relentlessly he perseveres, bullying her and almost taking possession of her life, allowing her to live only for her work. Eventually his ambition is achieved. Francesca's genius is recognized and she becomes a famous concert pianist.

When Francesca is older, she falls in love with a young American, played by Hugh McDermott. Her guardian finds out and forbids her to see him again, taking her away to the Continent to play in various concerts and never allowing her out of his sight. When they return to England, he engages an artist (Albert Lieven) to paint her portrait. The artist asks Francesca to run away with him. Nicholas discovers this and there is the famous scene that no one ever seems to forget, when he crashes his stick down on her hands while she is playing the piano and shouts: "If you won't play for me, you won't play for anyone else!"

Francesca runs away from him, but she and the artist get involved in a car accident and her hands are badly hurt. She believes the injury is the result of the stick and that she will never play again; she actually tries to play but has lost her confidence and gives up. Acute depression sets in and she attempts suicide by trying to drown herself. She is saved and sent to a sanatorium where the psychiatrist, played brilliantly by Herbert Lom, puts her under narco-hypnotic treatment. He explains how "the human mind is like Salome at the beginning of her dance hidden from the outside world by seven veils. Veils of reserve, of shyness, of modesty. With friends the average person will drop one veil, then another, maybe three or four altogether. With a lover he will take off five or even six, but never the seventh." He manages to cure her in the end by stripping away all the veils of her mind. This releases her from her guardian Nicholas's domination; they are reunited and both realize that they cannot do without each other and that it was love they had been fighting all along. Nicholas is successfully able to convince her that her talent and ability have not been lost.

The depth and impact of the film are difficult to describe, but my thanks will always go to Sidney and Muriel Box for the way they achieved this and for some of the brilliant ideas that made this film so outstanding. One of the magic moments is right in the beginning when Francesca in a flashback is running away at night from the hospital and Nicholas's domination, to the Serpentine in Kensington Gardens in order to try to commit suicide. She is in her nightdress and climbs up on the bridge ready to jump (at this moment a "double" actually took over). The scene has a beautiful dreamlike quality, as they filmed it in slow motion with the camera below shooting upward. She jumps and, with the nightdress billowing out around her, floats, like a wounded white bird, slowly down, down onto the water.

The first time I met James Mason was on the set before rehearsal. I was rather frightened of him, but fascinated. I thanked him politely for having saved the whole project and added that if ever I became a star it would be thanks to him and I would do anything for him in return. He answered: "I will hold you to that!"

We then started rehearsing the scene at the piano

where he hits my hands. I was playing, or rather pretending to, while James was walking up and down behind me, shouting his speech and working himself up for the crash of the stick on the keyboard. The director had asked me to keep my hands on the notes as long as possible before I withdrew them, to make it look realistic. The next thing we heard was the director shouting to us to lie on the floor. An unexploded bomb from the war had gone off outside. Things were flying about in the studio and dust and plaster were falling on us. After the danger was over, we were told to start rehearsing again. Returning to work probably saved our nerves, but what with the bomb exploding and James hitting me I can't think how my hands stayed on, or anywhere near, that piano.

James Mason is a marvelous actor. I was very lucky to play opposite him. He has, which is rare, an excitement about his personality—it's electric and sparks one off. We seemed chemically to work well together as screen personalities. I did the stage play of the film later with Leo Genn, but it didn't succeed nearly as well.

There are things about James I will always love. There is nothing show biz about him. He loves simple things and a simple life—his beautiful house in Switzerland facing the mountains proves that.

I remember strolling along empty streets with him in London on a Sunday—looking through the windows of closed shops, searching out old hidden streets full of history, walking in the rain, in old clothes, stopping suddenly and hearing, "Come here, Annie." James taking me in his arms and giving me an enormous hug for all to see.

I remember him trying to take a photograph of me and my dog, Whisky, sitting on a wall at Brighton, facing the sea. He was using one of those cameras with a time release, so he had to dash around in time to join me after setting it. We couldn't get it right; Whisky was growling, and I was laughing, and James was treating the whole episode as if he were filming in a Hollywood studio, which made me laugh all the more. And not one single person in the crowd walking past us along the waterfront even glanced at us. It always amazes me that people never seem to recognize actors and actresses, even after all the publicity and fame we get, if we are not in the setting they think of us in on the screen. We don't seem to exist unless it's in *their* world, and then it can be a rush for autographs. Of course nowadays it's different, as television has changed all this.

For the piano playing in the film I studied at the Royal College of Music for three months, not of course to play— Eileen Joyce did that brilliantly—but to learn how to cheat it all, without playing a note. The audience was taken in even though the camera was actually focused on my hands quite often. It was terribly hard work but I was well rewarded when I was filmed at the Albert Hall playing Rachmaninov's Piano Concerto No. 2 and Grieg's Concerto in A minor, all on a dummy piano, with the London Philharmonic Orchestra behind me and Muir Mathieson conducting; I was so excited I nearly cried at the end of the scene, when I came to the last chords of the Rachmaninov concerto. I felt I had really played it, and what an experience.

On my way to New York later, I received a cable sent to the boat asking if I would play the Grieg Concerto at a concert at Carnegie Hall. I wish I had had the cheek to do it and stand up just before the end, while the piano went on playing, off stage.

The film appeared first in New York; it was a smash hit and won an Oscar; later it came to London. Sidney Box did not want me to be all dressed up for the first night. He thought it would be more original if I arrived straight from the studios, so I turned up in a blue-and-white-striped woolen skirt, yellow woolen stockings and a shirt, with my blonde hair long and straight—which made its own success in the film—not looking at all the typical film star. We had tremendous notices and publicity from the press, and photographs in all the papers of me shopping, bicycling, gardening and painting, and of course details about the vast contract I had signed with Rank. There was great applause at the end of the film.

As I made my exit I had to step over a gentleman sitting by himself at the end of the row. He looked up at me and said, "Terribly disappointing, don't you think? I was so looking forward to it." Everyone swore he didn't recognize me in my strange get-up but I will always have a sneaking suspicion that he did.

I had the great honor just after the first night in London, of being asked to go to Marlborough House to a private showing of *The Seventh Veil* for Her Majesty Queen Mary. We were in a tiny cinema and I sat next to the queen in the front row. She had a rug placed over her knees and sat up very straight. A man in the audience a few rows back had a bad coughing fit. Queen Mary turned around very slowly with great dignity and gazed straight at him. It took two seconds flat, then there was a strangled gulp and silence. Slowly the Queen turned back and concentrated on the screen again. What happened to the man, I don't know. He probably died. She had tears in her eyes at the end of the film; she turned to me and said, "Child, you didn't go to that horrid man at the end, did you? I couldn't quite see without my glasses."

The next day a photograph of Her Majesty arrived by courier at my house. It was signed by the Queen: "It was a great pleasure to me to have seen your beautiful acting in *The Seventh Veil.*" I treasure this very much.

I met Queen Mary several times—once at a small lunch party given by Sir Louis Gregg, her equerry. He didn't tell me who was coming but said he would be very angry if I was late. In my work I seem only to be with men all the time, and as they automatically assume that women are late for everything I have trained myself to be sitting there, waiting for them when they arrive. Well, at least it helps to start the meeting off on the right foot.

We sat down, eight for lunch. I faced the queen. Sir Louis, after the coffee, asked me to tell Her Majesty a story I had told him. I didn't think it was at all appropriate, but Louis insisted, so I said: "My small daughter, Francesca, Ma'am, was asked by the headmistress at her kindergarten, 'What is your Mummy doing now?' Francesca answered promptly, 'Oh, Mummy is so tired because she is working very hard on the streets at night.'" The Queen, to my relief, laughed and laughed. I had been filming "night scenes" in a bustle and bonnet in Beauchamp Place with Ray Milland for Paramount Studios—for the film *So Evil My Love.*

The Seventh Veil had and still has the most extraordinary effect on the audience. A taxi driver only last week refused to take any money. He kept saying it would bring him bad luck and that he would never forget James Mason hitting me and even now he wanted to hit him back. One would have thought after more than thirty years it would be completely forgotten, considering all the cruelty and violence we see now on television; but no. It is strange how many people, young and old, react to this scene.

This film made me an international star overnight. It gave me, as I said, what at that time was an impressive contract of a million dollars with the Rank Organisation, one of the biggest amounts that had ever been paid in England.

CHAPTER 2

A Kind of Wonder

"The wind blows out of the gates of the day,
The wind blows over the lonely of heart,
And the lonely of heart is withered away."
The Land of Heart's Desire—W. B. YEATS

My birth was sudden and dramatic.

I was told that my parents were on their way from London to Banchory Lodge, Aberdeen, Scotland, when my mother at a most inconvenient moment en route started her labor pains. She was forced to break her journey and was taken to furnished rooms in Cheshire. I arrived prematurely on an ice-cold day in January.

A fire was hastily lit in the bedroom, and apparently a few moments after my birth the room caught fire. The fire spread and my mother and I were hurriedly bundled out of doors. I think they gave me up for dead, but I survived. I am not a Scot for nothing, though sadly I was born south of the Border. I agree with Compton Mac-Kenzie when he said that by accident he was English, by desire a Scot.

I didn't see my mother very much for the first few months of my life. She was ill and took some time to recuperate, so we returned to London for several months, and I was looked after by an unmarried aunt who adored me. Later on in my life I used to tease her and say I believed that she was really my mother. While appearing to be shocked, she secretly, I know, loved the suggestion. I called her Tanty; it was she, and only she, who made life endurable in the beginning, with her love and understanding.

Tanty was my mother's eldest sister. She was not married because in the days when she was young, near the turn of the century, the eldest unmarried daughter was expected to look after the family and run the house, in this case a large one in London. It was considered her duty.

My grandmother, at around forty, retired to her bed (on good days the sofa) with something the matter with her leg; she never got up again. She lay there holding court, looking helpless and fetching, in a black dress buttoned up to the neck with a large oval cameo at the throat. A white lace cap trimmed with black velvet ribbon covered her hair. She always seemed very remote and mysterious as she never came downstairs lower than the two top floors and we were all summoned up to her. I remember asking the cook if someone had cut off her legs as we never saw them. A light rug always covered her lower half.

Tanty for the rest of her life had to organize the household and make everyone in her large family of brothers and sisters happy—all except herself. She had been in love with a famous judge and he with her, but marriage was out of the question because of her "duties."

Tanty had a wonderful brain—several of my men friends used to say that they would rather take her out to dinner than anyone else as she was such a fascinating companion. This was when she was in her middle eighties. She had met Disraeli among others and I always felt was utterly wasted in this life, except that she gave love and her life to others.

My mother was insanely jealous of her sister, who though not as delicately pretty as herself had an incredible inner strength. Tanty was tall and straight as a tree and had a lovely smile that started slowly and then spread all over one, giving a feeling of warmth and safety. As far as I am concerned, Tanty was—and is now, wherever she is—my mother, at least in spirit.

I have never really believed the story about my birth. It still seemed shrouded in mystery and I have always assumed that my mother was not my real mother and that I was a "changeling" whom she was forced to adopt. But to this day I can give no reasonable answer to why I feel like this. She certainly never cared for me, and my life as a child was very unhappy.

I am not going to dwell on my childhood. It seems a waste of time to make a fuss over a small part at the beginning. After all, to be born one has to get into the world somehow, either in love, or, if there is a destiny to be fulfilled, through any circumstances that are available. Perhaps in the latter case one has to work harder to survive—who knows?

My father was rather an old father, and I never got to know him very well. He was a strange mixture really—a dreamer who knew a lot about art and, by contrast, also a great sportsman. He went to Fettes College in Scotland, and later played rugger for Scotland and Cambridge University and rowed for Clare College. But he was never a success in his life and hopeless at business. Perhaps my mother tried to push him too hard in her frustration at his apparent weakness. She certainly bullied and bossed him and he always seemed afraid of her. As I said, she was very pretty and had always been spoiled. Sadly, what I mostly remember were her incessant complaints about her life and her attitude towards me.

Religion played a big part in my mother's life. It was always church on Sunday, twice, and for her again in the middle of the week. Our cook said she wished Madam wouldn't go so often as she always came back so much worse. Mother and I definitely didn't see eye to eye about God. One day in church we nearly had a fight. I think she would have smacked me if we hadn't been sitting in the front pew. It was all to do with kneeling. Mother groveled to God—I preferred to kneel bolt upright and face Him. On this occasion we conversed in low whispers. "Ann, put your hands over your face and bow down, you are not being reverent." Me: "No. I don't think God likes it that way." Mother: "That is very wicked. How do you know what God wants?" Me: "I do, he's here." On that positive note my head was sharply pushed down on to the footstool and held there for a considerable time.

I didn't like church at all. But once, when praying, I was looking through my fingers and, to my astonishment, I saw the most beautiful picture forming slowly before my eyes. It was so beautiful that it is difficult to put into words. Everything in the church gradually seemed to melt into one radiant gold light: the cross, candles, the clergyman and choir, even the flowers had haloes of light around them. Everything was alive and moving. I shut my eyes then opened them again quickly. It was all still happening, only this time the people had faded out into a blue mist and the rest was shimmering and dancing. I wanted suddenly to cry.

My family have never seemed very real to me and I look quite unlike any of them. I have one brother and my mother adored and spoiled him as a child. He had red curls and bright blue eyes and was rather beautiful. I had straight hair and was plain. My mother kept saying: "For goodness' sake smile, child, and take away that dour Scottish expression."

My brother is now a well-known and successful playwright. He writes with his wife, Kay Bannerman, the former actress, under the name of Harold Brooke, and their plays are extremely funny. I admire them very much, as comedy and farce are much more difficult to write than tragedy—and the same goes for acting. We have gone our different ways over the years and we don't see much of each other.

I am descended from William Hogarth, the painter, on my father's side, and at one time we had his palette and brush in the family. Now they have been given to the Victoria and Albert Museum. The family was rather ashamed of our famous ancestor. They considered his caricatures and satires of English life vulgar and coarse and frowned on his "Rake's Progress" and "Gin Alley."

When my father visited China, he was asked to find out what had happened to long-lost Uncle George, another Hogarth and a black sheep of the family who had disappeared years back in history somewhere in that country. My father came home with the news that Uncle George had indeed gone to China with four friends to pillage graves and steal the ancestral gold and silver. They had traveled in a ship that had guns sticking out either side. One night they had landed and dug up their loot. When they returned to the ship in the dark, they found that the tide had gone out and the ship was on its side. One lot of guns was buried in the sand; the other lot was facing up to heaven. They were stuck. The Chinese caught them and ordered Uncle George and his friends to dig their graves. They then cut off their heads. So ended Uncle George, and the Hogarths sank again into shame.

I remember only one important conversation with my father. We were walking on the heath in Scotland, at Deeside; I was holding his hand and was skipping along unbelievably happy. It had been raining and the road looked as if it had been washed with a brush dipped in purple paint, a reflection from the heather all around us. The sky was wild and passionate. I wore my kilt and felt proud to be a Scot, and the wind was blowing us up the hill.

"Lassie," said my father, "now you are seven—that magic number to arrive at—you must ask yourself as you climb a hill, 'When I get to the top, what will I see?' You must always feel the excitement and want to know what is beyond, then you will never grow old. Promise me, lassie?"

I didn't understand, but I flung my arms around his neck and promised.

It is a strange instinct that compels a child to suppress what it feels should be hidden, so very few people know what happened in my childhood except, of course, Tanty.

I often wonder why, after all these years, certain incidents still stand out to me as rather cruel and difficult to understand. I was always being punished in one way or another. But one memorable day I shouted at Mother in fury, and she reported me to my father and insisted on his spanking me. I don't know who was more embarrassed, Father or me. We went solemnly to the study; neither of us knew how to begin. It became a clumsy, comical scene and finished up with me across his knees, in fits of giggles, being gently smacked on my bottom. After it was over Father left hurriedly to play golf. Mother was very cross because I didn't cry.

Three things happened when I was very small that distressed me terribly.

One night my father and mother were going out to dinner and my mother came to the nursery to say good night. She passed by my bed, went over to my brother, picked him up and hugged him. I remember the room. He was sleeping in the corner near a window and there were a few pictures of animals around the walls. One was of a rabbit over my bed, whom I called Thumper and used to talk to by the hour.

My mother tucked my brother up and I held my breath. Would she come to me this time? I imagined her leaning over me, the smell of the violets pinned to her dress and her hand stroking my hair. I lay there waiting and hoping. Then she turned, walked toward the door and switched off the lights—nothing but darkness remained and my usual storm of tears.

I tried desperately to win her love, but I failed and after overhearing a conversation outside the door when my mother was chattering to a friend, I decided once and for all that I didn't belong to her. I was a changeling, as in the fairy tales that were read to me, and Father had found me and had asked my mother to look after me.

The friend said to my mother: "How is your child, Mrs. Todd?" My mother answered: "Adorable as ever and I am so proud of him." The guest lowered her voice and whispered: "And the other?" "Still as impossible as ever; it's a great burden to me," said my mother.

And then another incident when I was around eight or nine years old. I had always been told that only people who *loved* each other kissed on the mouth (like Mummies and Daddies). I loved the milkman, so I flung my arms around his neck and kissed him—he reciprocated. I then dashed into the kitchen where my mother was cutting up

apples. In a loud and excited voice I said: "Mummy, I
have just been kissed." My mother whirled round, knife
in hand, and said sharply: "On the mouth?" I answered:
"Yes, and I like it." She came very close to me—she was
trembling—and then she whispered: "So—now you will
have a baby."

   That little scene haunted me for a long time and slowed
down any sex that happened to be there to a snail's pace.
I could not understand what she meant and crept around
in secret panic waiting for the birth.

Soon it was decided that the family were to leave Scotland
and live permanently in London. I was utterly heartbroken and stayed in one of my black moods for days on
end. I think the excuse was Mother's health; Aberdeen
can be wickedly cold.

   But now it was spring and the air was soft. "Brooding
weather" when one feels all nature is thinking out the
next move and keeping it secret for the moment. My
mother and I were walking down a country lane. There
was a soft wind blowing. I have always loved the wind. It
has been a great friend to me all through my life. When it
is fierce and passionate it seems to be ordering me to fight
on with courage. When it is soft and gentle I feel love and
understanding, and its sensuous touch always excites
me.

   On this day there were primroses banked high on
either side of the lane. I remember that I was wearing a
cotton frock and I had black shoes and stockings on and a
little coral necklace that my father had brought back from
one of his many travels abroad. My tight pigtails stuck out
like sticks underneath a floppy straw hat. I remember it
all so clearly, like seeing the whole scene reflected and
moving in a mirror. My mother was walking ahead of me.

Then, I remember quite clearly, I met an angel. I saw a tall man dressed in a long white robe with a light all round him walking toward us. As he passed he smiled at me, then he faded into the trees. I asked my mother why she hadn't said "Good morning" to him. She was so strict about manners, but she answered: "What man?" and gave me that look that said, "You have been lying again." But *I* knew I had met my guardian angel.

Of course everything is forgiven now between Mother and me, through my prayers, I hope. And Mother, wherever she is, must be laughing at the situations which I turned into great dramas. Had she been alive now, I am sure someone would have found the answer to her obvious unhappiness and to the pattern of rejection that has always haunted me, though at long last I have broken it. I believe in reincarnation so perhaps my mother and I had to meet in this life to work out something that needed to be repaid from a previous existence. I wonder if we succeeded. I wonder.

When we arrived in London we stayed in a furnished flat and were bidden to Grandfather's large house facing Kensington Gardens for lunch on most Sundays. How I dreaded those lunches. He would balance a piece of mouse cheese on a small biscuit, then look around the table, usually choosing me as the stupidest of his grandchildren, and say: "Now, Ann, you can have this if you tell me what was the color of the wedding dress of Queen Elizabeth I."

All the other children tittered—I was puce in the face. "White, Granddad," I stammered.

"No, stupid child," he answered. "She was never married. But perhaps you can tell me this: the color of Gulliver's black horse?"

"No, Granddad," I murmured.

"*Black* horse, *black* horse, child." Everyone giggled.

When I stayed there sometimes for weekends with him and Grandma, we all had to be down for prayers every morning sharp at nine o'clock—a gong rang. Everyone had to attend—cook, housemaids, all the staff. We would kneel facing our chairs, our bottoms facing Granddad, who sat comfortably at the dining room table reading out prayers, gospels and collects, while cook fidgeted—praying that the breakfast wasn't burning in the kitchen.

The time before prayers was the most exciting moment for me because I was allowed to get into Tanty's bed while she dressed and play with a set of little brass bowls with scarlet centers that fitted into each other, getting smaller and smaller. I can see myself now, curled up under the eiderdown chattering away like a small magpie to the only person I loved in the whole wide world. I remember the utter bliss of those moments—watching Tanty move around the room and seeing her reflection in the mirror as she pinned up her hair; the cold feeling that made me shiver when I pressed the golden bowls against my face; and hearing again and again the story that they had come from a place called Burma, far, far away—the magic of it all.

Once I said to Tanty: "Why can't I come and live with you?" "Because, my kitten, you have a Mummy and Daddy and you belong to them," she answered.

I climbed off the bed and crept up behind her. *"No I don't,"* I said fiercely. "I belong to *you. Please, please,* let me stay with you forever."

She caught me up in her arms and covered my face with kisses. The moment the gong rang it broke our secret togetherness and we came down to earth as we descended to the dining room for prayers—perhaps we felt a little guilty.

I loved Grandma and Grandfather's house. It had long passages in the basement where the kitchens were and where we were allowed to dash up and down and make as much noise as we liked, and lots of staircases that led up to the top floor where the "servants" slept—a very long climb from the basement. In between all this there was a hydraulic chair on rails that ran up and down the side of the staircase to convey in slow grandeur my grandmother from her bedroom to the loo on the floor below, while her personal maid waited outside, ready to waft her back again. It had gears—"Go" and "Stop," gadgets, etc.—and all children were strictly forbidden to touch it. I once broke the rule and, not knowing how to put on the brake, hurtled down two floors and was thrown on my head outside the conservatory where Tanty was watering some ferns. She grabbed me and spirited me away to her room where she put plaster on my face—but there was a rumpus all the same.

The drawing room was spacious and grand and had a pianola. When Grandmother's mind was failing she often sent for a grandchild to play to her some new piece learned at school; she never knew that we just switched on the pianola. The keys hopped up and down by themselves and out came Beethoven and Brahms. She always said at the end: "You played very well, my child— but work, hard *work* is the answer." This was said to me when I was around six!

The most fascinating things in that room for me were the two enormous marble statues at either end of the mantelpiece. They were figures of two cherubs, their elbows on their knees, thinking deeply. I loved them passionately. I don't know why I had this feeling that I knew them so well. Tanty told me later that the first time she caught me talking to them she was astonished. I must have been about four years old. She opened the door and saw me alone in the room, standing with my back to her, my arms clasped behind me, my head on one side, gazing up at them. I was talking loudly in the most extraordinary language (not baby talk). She said it sounded like Chinese. Then I would pause, nod my head as if listening, or start arguing. Sometimes I laughed as if at some joke, and once she caught me crying with my hands over my face. But always it was the same language, spoken as if I were an adult having an interesting conversation, and with an uncanny concentration.

She asked me once, very gently, why I was talking to them, but I never told her—not even her—except to say, "They are my friends." I continued my conversations for many years whenever I went to stay with her. Perhaps the cherubs were being used by the invisible world, almost like a private telephone, to chat to me; who knows? Looking back on these conversations I have often wondered whether children who have had to go through a certain amount of insecurity and loneliness are perhaps compensated in this sort of way to help them in their need. They are as children naturally more open to that help and comfort which is available to us all if only we are willing to receive it. I think I have always accepted with a kind of wonder what comes to me from sources which I do not necessarily have to understand.

Tanty left one cherub to me in her will, my favorite, but I never got it. Perhaps it was right—it would have been a shame to separate them from each other.

Only below stairs did I feel really at home when Tanty was away. I will always remember Jane, the much-loved cook, as I begged her to let me stay and not go home, wiping away my tears as she brushed my hair, then sending me back above ground again.

Much later on, when I was sixteen, I remember Jane's tenderness when she found me sobbing into my pillow one night, clutching a dance program with "John" written down for every dance. A handsome Gordon Highlander, he had returned to Scotland and his regiment without saying goodbye. I knew definitely that my life was finished.

CHAPTER 3

This Way to the Lemonade

I was sent to a boarding school in Eastbourne at a very early age for that time—I was not quite eleven years old and by far the youngest in the school.

One night soon after I arrived I was found sleepwalking. It created such a drama that I decided to "act" it next time. I floated down the dormitory, hands outstretched, went over the windowsill, through the window, onto the roof. The fire engine had to be summoned, but I played to a most appreciative audience.

One time Miss Gilling-Lax, the headmistress, sent for me and talked *at* me so severely that I immediately enclosed myself in a pink-colored cloud while her voice floated below me. It concerned a new girl from Australia who had just arrived. She was in my dormitory and we had been asked to be kind to her as she was homesick. She cried so much the first night that none of us could sleep, so I took her into my bed to cuddle her and make her feel loved. Next day notices were on the school board: "Any girl found in the bed of another girl will be dismissed immediately."

I stayed in my cloud for many years—no one explained—and it just seemed odd that as one wasn't allowed to get into bed with a boy and now not with a girl, whom could you love, and where?

Without meaning to, I always seemed to get caught up in drama, and still do. My daughter has inherited this from me. Her conversations on the telephone to me invariably start: "Ma—guess *what?*" Then follows an incredible story which would only happen to most people once in a lifetime if they were lucky.

Even running in a Girl Guide race as a Brownie, and coming in last, I got all the attention as I ran with my mouth open and a wasp got in. Everyone dashed to me and tried to scoop out the terrified wasp with a spoon, while the girl who had won stood unnoticed and alone.

Confirmation was not a success really; although I remember I did have an eager desire to become a nun. I think I was too young and never took in what it was all about. I walked up the aisle of the church with the other girls, whose veils reached to their waists. As I was very small, mine was too long and made me look like a bride. I was under the impression that I was going to be able to speak French—"Be filled with the Holy Ghost and begin to speak with other tongues." The bishop's hand came down heavily on my head and I whispered to myself, *"Je suis, tu es, il est,"* got stuck, felt let down and started to cry. So instead of making my exit radiant and calm with the other girls, I sniveled all the way down the aisle with head bowed, no handkerchief and wondering if I dared use my veil.

My only appearance as an actress in the school play was also a flop. I was chosen, as a great honor, to be a slave, with a black face, to Portia in *The Merchant of Venice,* and carry her train. (I had a passionate crush on her at the time.) We were standing outside the gym waiting for our entrance when I said, "I'm going to be sick."

The gym mistress whirled around on me. "You are *not,*" she said.

"What's the matter with you?"

I answered, "I'm so nervous."

She snapped back, *"You* nervous. No one is going to look at *you*—they will be looking at *Portia.*"

I *was* sick.

I made one other appearance, this time at the school concert—which was a disaster. My father was a very good musician. He used to play the piano sometimes in the evenings when I was in bed and I would leave my door open and listen to my favorite piece, an arrangement of Schubert's "Erl-King" that made me tremble with excitement over the wickedness and evil of it all. Father made it very plain to me and everyone else that he hoped and expected that his daughter would be a good pianist. So, when I went to my boarding school it was arranged for me to have long and boring lessons with the most unattractive lady whose fingers went up and down like stiff soldiers, while she hummed the tune through clenched teeth.

I was no good at anything at school, except that by virtue of being lefhanded, I made things difficult for everyone else at games (this went for cricket as I used to be bowled out first ball and the field, very bored, had to change back again immediately for a righthanded batswoman) and I remained most of my school life at the bottom of the class—but I did like reading poetry.

For the concert, as Father and Mother would be there with other parents, I was told I was to play the Chopin Prelude in A. I sat at the back of the hall trying to hide away. My hands were clammy. I felt sick. When my name was called I prayed to be allowed to faint. I sat down at the piano that seemed to envelop me and started to play. Seven seconds after the beginning my fingers became numb and my mind seemed to float away. I stopped and murmured, "I'm sorry."

"Start again, please," said the headmistress. I started again. The same thing happened. I stood up.

"Sit down, child, and concentrate—try again," she said.

The third time was just another repetition of the agony. I left the hated piano and ran back through the audience to my seat, my hand covering my face, crying with shame.

This experience affected me for the future more than people knew. When we were filming the scene of me as a child in the film of *The Seventh Veil* and I had to play the piano and break down, I re-enacted (even in a gym tunic!) the same struggle with the same Chopin and the same feeling of utter failure as I had had all those years ago at school. After this the piano was abandoned and poetry took its place, though not facing an audience. I love music and drown my cottage in it most of the day when I am there and strum on my guitar, but I still suffer agony when attending a concert—for the pianist—until she or he has got through the first few minutes, then I can relax.

I left school early and Mother had me back on her hands again and was determined now to "bring me out" as a debutante in London society and marry me to a duke. I fought it tooth and nail. The result was spots and an enveloping rash on my neck and chest. But Mother won—apart from the duke.

My first sortie as a budding debutante was most interesting—Mother was so afraid I wouldn't go at the last moment that she despatched me in a taxi much too early. The party was being given for young people—dinner and dancing at Lady B.'s grand house. I arrived more than half an hour too soon. The butler opened the door. I shook hands and followed him upstairs into an enormous room full of gilt chairs and large mirrors which I, in my nervousness, thought were swinging backward and forward. He took my velvet cloak and told me to sit down. Then, looking down his nose, he said, "Her ladyship will not be down for some time yet—I will inform her you are here."

Her ladyship must have been furious at my arrival, but she took her time and then descended. She opened the door; the room was empty. Then she saw a pair of feet sticking out from behind the sofa. I heard afterward that she screamed. I had fainted. The butler was sent for and they poured water over me. As I sat there, drenching wet, Lady B. telephoned my mother, who answered immediately that I was to stay where I was as she was determined that I should get over my nerves—no one was to "give way" to me. I was immensely sorry for Lady B. and even more for myself.

Later on in the season I was sent off to my first grownup "do" in the country. I think it was held at the duke and duchess of Devonshire's house, and this time I was chaperoned by Tanty, who happened to know the duchess. I was dressed all in white—whitespangled short dinner dress, white stockings, white shoes, white gloves and an enormous frosted white orchid on my right shoulder.

We sat down to dinner in a beautiful room lit by candles, and the gentleman next to me opened the conversation by saying, "What are you—a sacrificial lamb?" He was *wildly* attractive—not young like the rest of our party, but at least twenty-five—and very attentive. I found out afterward he was having an affair with a very chic sophisticated lady sitting opposite us. They had had a row, so his attention to me was intended to make her jealous.

At the end of dinner the footmen carried around the table large gorgeous bowls of fruit, each looking like a Dutch still life. Everyone murmured approval, and only the bravest took a nut. It got to me—I took a large orange just as the duchess was getting to her feet to take the ladies out and leave the men to their port. She sat down again while I chewed my way through the orange, quite oblivious to what was happening. Everyone waited. The smell of the orange completely obliterated the Patou, Dior and other scents as it wafted around the table.

After dinner we started dancing. Kit, my wildly attractive gentleman, suggested we go to his flat nearby and listen to some records. I said, "How lovely, I will go and tell Tanty." He got around that one and bundled me into an open sports car. I remember the thrill, driving at night through the lanes with the wind blowing my hair and knowing with complete assurance that he loved me and that I had a mad passion for him. We arrived. He promptly turned out most of the lights, saying it would be more cozy. I flopped on the floor. He opened a bottle of champagne and I sat gazing at him in wonder. He then leaned forward to hand me a glass, and I saw a different look in his eye. He touched my hand and I fainted.

I came to in the kitchen, my head in the sink and water being poured on me yet again. My wildly attractive gentleman was in a panic and very cross. He drove me hastily back to the dance and didn't look at me again—I was heartbroken. I was sure he loved me and that I would marry him and live happily ever after.

Of course I was a goose and, let's face it, rather stupid. No one would believe all this now.

But oh! how innocent we were and how strictly protected—from what?

My debutante period was short-lived. The spots didn't help and no one seemed to care enough to try to cure them. I did not attract a duke. I hated shopping for the "right" clothes, having my hair done and going to dances where I usually stood against the wall with my dance program hanging limply from my wrist, praying that my guardian angel would force some young man to save me and ask me to dance. It was all agony, including Mother's questions when I returned home about whom I had met and whether I had been a success. I always answered that I had.

Things went from bad to worse as I struggled on. Mother became desperate and I broke down under the strain. I got paler and paler, cried a great deal and couldn't eat. It was extraordinary; the moment I was asked out to a meal my throat closed up and I felt sick. No one who has not experienced this can know what a torture it is. I used to enter the dining room and look anxiously at all the knives and forks laid out on the table; if there was only one of each I could struggle through by hiding most of the food under the salad, but if there were rows of shining spoons and fish knives, etc., I would immediately make some excuse about not feeling well and nibble a roll and butter all through the meal, embarrassing everyone.

Then suddenly everything changed. A new doctor was called in who must have been very advanced for his time, and he insisted that I work hard, become exhausted and so forget myself. At the same time my mother ran into an old friend of hers whose daughter had been at my boarding school and, when she left, had gone to dramatic and speech training school in London and then on to the stage. She is now the well-known actress Alison Leggatt. Her mother suggested this might be a good idea for me— not to go on the stage, that was out of the question, but to take the three-year course with a diploma at the end for teaching speech training and elocution.

Dressed in a garment that resembled a gym tunic and looking years younger than my just seventeen years, I went with my mother for an interview with the head of the Central School of Speech Training and Dramatic Art at the Royal Albert Hall. The lecture rooms and tiny theater were around the edge of the building with the hall in the center.

The head was Miss Elsie Fogerty. She was a frightening lady. She was short and plump and had wispy gray hair usually hanging down over her collar. She always wore a long black skirt which hung unevenly showing a large piece of white petticoat. She seemed always to be munching an apple. When she met students in the corridor she was apt to put her hand firmly on their diaphragms and command them to take a big breath and let it out slowly, intoning, "AH—EH—EE—OH—OU." She certainly produced some wonderful voices. Laurence Olivier was a student there. Peggy Ashcroft and many other famous people studied under her dominating but brilliant tuition.

At my interview I sat dumb while Mother started on a long monologue. Miss Fogerty silenced her and gazed at me. "She is too young," she said firmly. "She knows nothing. It would be a waste of my time to teach her. Yes, a waste of my time. Anyway, she will get married young—much more suitable." She then gave me a long look and added, "Bring her back in six months if she grows up."

We left the Albert Hall and walked out into a damp cold autumn day and as I climbed onto the bus with my mother I thought, "Perhaps I will never grow up and remain a stunted dwarf with a Scottish expression and no mind for the rest of my life."

At the end of six months I returned to Miss Fogerty, this time alone, with lipstick on, a new hairdo and a large woolen scarf wound twice around my neck hiding most of my face but—I thought, after much consideration—looking artistic and nonchalantly sophisticated. To my surprise I was "passed."

Then came the dramatic entrance exam which all students had to do. I can't remember what I had to recite but I do remember it entailed rolling about on the floor in agony and screaming so hard that I must have nearly removed the roof of the Albert Hall. There were two other tests. For one we had to go on the stage individually and open a telegram handed to us and react to what it said. Mine was something like: "Your mother has had an accident—has dropped down dead." I had no idea what to do, so I doubled up with laughter and rocked backward and forward in my mirth. I passed, perhaps because I was more original than the others.

The last test was really advanced and taught me a lesson I have never forgotten. We were told to sit alone on a hard chair in the middle of the stage facing the footlights. A bright light was focused on one's face. Beyond were a few important people staring at one out of the blackness and absolute silence which went on and on—no one moved. The test was to see if the student could feel and act being alone and ignore the audience. After a few moments of this silence the natural reaction was to fidget, cross and recross one's legs, look desperately into the wings and call out into the blackness of the stalls beyond, "What am I meant to *do*?" To be an actress it is essential to be relaxed and forget that people are staring at you, be real and never fidget or be self-conscious. Let the audience be the voyeurs. I had been let into the secret before the test and so managed, by clinging to the chair, to sit like a rock, hardly breathing, staring back at the examiners in the darkness—I passed!

We were all frightened of Miss Fogerty. After all these years I remember how I dreaded those Saturday morning recitation classes which she taught. I used to get into the back row and double up with my head down so that she couldn't see me. One day she called me out. I stood on the little raised platform with my hands clenched behind my back. I started:

"When the hounds of spring are on winter's traces
    The mother of months in—"

"Stop," shouted Miss Fogerty. "Start again. I can't hear you." It was a small room and she was only a few feet away, sitting at her desk, munching her apple. I raised my voice:

"When the hounds of spring are on winter's traces
    The mother—"

"Don't shout, dear," she said, and then, "Will everyone leave the room, please? I wish to take Todd on her own." She called me this as there were so many Anns that term.

We were left alone. Miss Fogerty then rose up, grabbed my arm in a terrifying grip and dragged me around and around the room, repeating the lines over and over again. "Can't you hear the rhythm, child—the horses' feet?" She stamped her own and shouted: "Repeat after me: 'When the *hounds* of spring are on *winter's* traces, the *mother* of months in meadow or plain . . . '"

On she went relentlessly, tramping around that small room, shouting the rhythm at me and pulling me along with her. I burst into tears. She stopped abruptly and pulled me around to face her. "Now," she said in her natural marvelous voice. "*Now* you may be an actress whatever anyone says. Go away and *think* and *feel,* child."

We worked terribly hard, but I loved it all. We had fencing lessons, Greek dancing, mime, voice production, and history of costumes through the ages. Those students studying to be teachers, as I was, were put into the small parts of the plays that the dramatic students were doing. They definitely looked down on us. The men students apart from learning to act also came to the school to learn about direction. That's how I met George More O'Ferrall. George was rather fond of me. He was learning to be a director, which, of course, in later life he became and so successfully. I was enjoying the attentions of another student and got bored with George following me around.

Then one day during the end-of-term performance of *Prunella* by Laurence Housman, I was playing Pierrette to George's Pierrot. George was up a tree on the stage. My lines were: "Pierrot, come down. Pierrot, lift up your head. Pierrot, they said that you did not remember me at all. Yet out of my dreams I heard you call my name, and when you called I came."

It was too much for George. He fell out of the tree. He then hurried over to me and, instead of giving me a stylized peck of a kiss on my forehead, he firmly grasped me in his arms and planted a long passionate one on my lips. When he released me it got a big laugh. His Pierrot makeup with the large clown's mouth was now enveloping my face in a big red circle. When we got off the stage I smacked his face. Later I did many plays with George, including *Camille* and *The Vortex*.

As teaching students we did very little acting, so apart from *Prunella* I played First Lord in *As You Like It*, which wasn't exactly type casting, except perhaps for Peter Pan in the future, as I stood manlike, legs wide apart, the whole way through the play. Then *Naboth's Vineyard* by Clemence Dane, a brilliant and intellectual play for mostly men to act in. We played it with all women. King Ahab was a girl called Daisy. For some reason there were twelve slaves in the play representing twelve hours. I was the twelfth. We all wore pillow cases. I entered last in my pillow case with my thin arms sticking out either side. The moment I got on the stage I had to turn my back on the audience and waddle up to Daisy (Ahab) who naturally was up stage on her throne, so no one really ever saw me. I then went down on my knees, my bottom in the air, and intoned the following lines. (I must explain that being a Scot I have a little trouble pronouncing my double O's.)

> "Blind was I born and dark my hour
> But yet I died in *munlight*."

I was about to get up and waddle off, when I heard a

voice (Miss Fogerty's) from the audience consisting of teachers, examiners, friends and fellow students. "The word is moon, Todd, not *mun*." I turned still on my knees and looked back at the audience.

I said, "I beg your pardon?"

"Moooon, child, as in moo cow," came out of the darkness. "Go back and do it again."

In a daze I crossed the stage and approached Daisy for the second time; bowing low to her, I said,

> "Blind was I born and dark my hour
> But yet I died in moooo cow light."

I think it was the biggest laugh I have ever had in the theater, which is rather sad as it was unintentional but well timed!

Later I was given the part of Francesca da Rimini in *Paolo and Francesca,* the tragic Italian story of two young lovers put to death in 1289. Francesca is brought from the convent to marry the cruel tyrant Giovanni, but he sends his young brother Paolo to collect her and they fall in love. Later their love becomes known and they are killed.

This play influenced me a great deal. In later life I called myself Francesca in the film of *The Seventh Veil,* and I called my daughter Francesca. When I started making my own diary documentary films a few years ago I changed slightly these lovely lines of Paolo to Francesca: "So still it is that one can almost hear the sigh of all the lovers in the world and all the rivers running to the sea" to "So still it is that one can almost hear the heartbeat of the world." That was when we were filming Delphi at night, and when we were filming in the desert of Jordan I changed it to: "So still it is that one can almost hear the birth pangs of a new beginning."

In the last year of my course at the Albert Hall destiny stepped in and settled the next phase of my life. Two days before the first night of a play opening in the Arts Theatre Club in London an actress became ill and there was no understudy. The producer frantically rang up all the drama schools to find someone who might know the words. All they could find was me—a student studying to be a teacher. I just happened to know the words of the play as we had studied it in class. So they grabbed me and I was rushed to the theater. This was my first appearance on a professional stage.

The play was *The Land of Heart's Desire* by Yeats and I played the Faery Child. I seem always to be given wonderful entrances for any play or film I have done, but this, my first, was so lovely and to me so real that it had nothing to do with acting. I was just privileged to be there. In fact, the audience didn't seem to exist till someone coughed and broke my belief that I had just floated down from the sky. First I was heard singing off stage:

> "The wind blows out of the gates of the day,
> The wind blows over the lonely of heart,
> And the lonely of heart is withered away."

Then I made my entrance, coming through the mist of the forest as a spirit from another world, dressed in rags like green leaves, with bare feet and wearing a long wig the color of moonlight. I then went into the warm, earthy cottage of the Irish family. The priest in the play asked, "Child, how old are you?" And I answered, "Who can tell when I was born for the first time?"

I had had only two days of hectic rehearsals before the opening. My performance must have been strange in more ways than one, and the critics, either bored or stunned, gave me marvelous notices. For the first and last time I wasn't nervous and really rather enjoyed myself. I think the director must have been very clever as it was too late to teach me anyway so he just left me alone.

After this my father returned me to the school to continue my three-year teachers' course and I wasn't allowed to accept the $15 salary for my week's work. I later scraped through my diploma for teaching and left the Albert Hall. My student days had been the happiest of my life. Now I was back home again and had to find a job. The stage was never discussed, of course, but I was strong and full of hope and every morning when I woke up I used to say "Claim a miracle."

Then, out of the blue, a vague cousin of mine called Geoffrey, who was years older than myself, arrived back from India. He was very solid and had something to do with the army. Geoffrey, surprised to find that the child whom he had last seen with pigtails had grown into a fairly presentable young woman, announced he would like to marry me and take me back to India. Mother was very keen on this idea. I sank into a black depression and panic. When, later in a taxi, Geoffrey asked permission to kiss me and I said "No" but he caught hold of me, planted wet kisses on me and we landed on the floor, I knew it was a desperate moment in my life, which had to be settled immediately. So I went for a long walk in Kensington Gardens and asked my guardian angel to guide me. Then it seemed out of the air I heard the words, "Go to Uncle Bill."

Uncle Bill was my father's youngest brother and my favorite uncle. He had been a big game hunter and wrote a book called *Tiger, Tiger* under the name of Hogarth Todd. He was also a well-known polo player, especially in India. He married Aunt Molly, whom no one liked. I remember that whenever her name was mentioned the grown-ups lowered their voices as if she had committed a murder. I think her only sin must have been that she was too flighty for our heavy Scottish family and they disapproved of her looks.

Uncle Bill was on his honeymoon when, as he and his bride were walking through some jungle in India, a tigress protecting her young leaped at him unexpectedly. As Uncle Bill didn't have his gun, he was thrown on his back and badly mauled; in fact it left him paralyzed and a pathetic invalid for the rest of his life. The tigress was shot and the scowling skull hung over the door in our hall till my father died—true Todd Celtic retribution.

Aunt Molly left him. In his desperation Uncle Bill turned to the spirit world for help and healing. Of course the family strongly disapproved. My father for years had insisted that I should visit him regularly and cheer him up. I didn't understand what it was that my uncle believed in so intensely, but when I started to get dark circles under my eyes Father asked me about our conversations.

I told him that Uncle Bill had asked if I would agree to his getting in touch with me after he had died to prove that there is life after death—a continuation—and there should be no fear. I told Father that of course I had agreed; I thought it was a marvelous idea. I secretly saw myself chatting to my guardian angel. That ended abruptly my tea sessions with my favorite uncle.

But a seed had been sown for the future, and somewhere in the back of my mind I felt if ever I wanted to talk to Uncle Bill, all I had to do was to put a sort of long distance call through to him; it all seemed quite simple.

It was my last visit to him before he died, and I was pouring out my tale of woe about marriage to Geoffrey, sitting on the floor in floods of tears in front of the fire, when the door opened and a man came into the room. He looked down at me and said, "Well, Bill, what's happening here? What distress, most dramatic! The young lady should be an actress."

I looked up—I didn't know then—at Ian Hay, the famous author and playwright. Through my tears I blurted out, "I have got to marry someone and go to India."

Ian Hay answered, "What a silly idea. You should be on the stage. We are missing your great histrionic talents." Then he recognized me. Out of all the theaters in London he had strolled into the Arts Theatre Club to a matinée of *The Land of Heart's Desire* and seen my performance.

After that events moved very quickly. Ian Hay persuaded my father to let me "walk on" in one of his plays called *A Damsel in Distress,* and for a whole year I had one line to speak—"This way to the lemonade."

About this time I met David Niven. I was playing a small part in a play in the theater. David, who was then in the Highland Light Infantry—one of our famous Scottish regiments—came to see it and tried very hard to meet me. I became prim and proper and refused vehemently to have anything to do with him till he was properly introduced. He came every night for a week to see the play and to receive the answer "no" from the stage doorkeeper. Then on the last night he appeared in my dressing room with a broad grin of victory on his face—he had the author of the play introduce us! I was really cross, but due to this we started a long and lovely friendship.

He used to carry around in his wallet a terrible

snapshot of me looking ga-ga and, if I remember correctly (it was so long ago), wearing my hair in braids. The photograph was not kept next to his heart because of a romance between us but, as he explained to me, to save him if he got into a difficult situation with some girlfriend. He only had to draw it out of his pocket and say, "Oh, sorry, I forgot to tell you—this is my fiancé." I believe it traveled with him everywhere. Well it's nice to think I accomplished something, however unconsciously, in those early days. David has helped me a lot in my life and given me marvelous advice. I think I was able to help him too, especially after the tragic death of his first wife. I flew out from New York to Hollywood to be near him.

He used to call me Todd Epic. At this time in my youth I was going through a period of being rather grand and choosy, playing hard to get and expecting to be driven in Bentleys and Rolls Royces. As a great gesture David took me to dinner at the Café de Paris in London, which was very smart and *the* place to go. (Later, during the war and the Battle of Britain it received a direct hit from the Germans and nearly everyone was killed while they were having supper and dancing. That night of horror always haunts me as several of my friends were there at that time.)

David started to order dinner and he must have wilted as I happily chose the most expensive items on the menu: oysters . . . Champagne . . . asparagus. At the end of the evening he sent me home alone by taxi, which annoyed me considerably. I didn't know till much later on that the hotel had insisted that he stay there. And for three days he worked in the kitchens—washing up—because he couldn't pay the bill.

I remember one day he said to me, "Todd Epic, I have been thinking. Give me your advice—shall I leave the army and become an actor?"

I threw back my head and looking down my nose said, "*You* an *actor*, Niven? Of course not, don't be silly. I just can't see you being serious ever. You couldn't even say the line 'I love you' without being funny."

How wrong I was! Thank *goodness* he didn't listen to me or we might have lost a marvelous actor and a great personality.

So—because someone fell ill and the gap had to be filled, and because I didn't want to marry Geoffrey and go to India, and because I demanded guidance and claimed a miracle, I got what I don't think I really wanted. The pattern of destiny is very strange. I sometimes wonder why I had to be an actress and achieve a well-known name—when deep down I am a private person and rather like being alone. But as I often quote, or rather misquote, to myself:

> Damn! at last I've found out what I am
> I'm a creature that moves
> In predestined grooves
> Not a bus or car—but a *tram*.

Meaning . . . as long as you are on the right lines like a tram, then all is well. Life is worked out for all of us by the powers-that-be and you can either do it their way or yours.

CHAPTER 4

The Raising of the Curtain

F rom then on I was able to call myself an actress. My father and mother did not approve and they suggested that I change my name, but after I had made a success this was all forgotten. I was in several plays, usually playing the ingénue; the management paid more for my clothes than they paid for me. I flitted through various comedies and made one or two films and felt things were going fairly well. Then one night, while being driven along the Portsmouth road in the rain, I had a bad car accident. My face was very badly cut and they had to put clips on it before taking me by ambulance back to London and Tanty. The doctor came with us, and when we arrived, with me on a stretcher and covered with a sheet, poor Tanty thought I was dead.

At 4:30 A.M. the well-known surgeon McIndoe arrived. He came into the bedroom, took my hands in his and told me they were going to take off the bandages and that I might not be able to see, as both eyes could be affected, but that I was to trust him completely. I lay there, listening to his confident voice, so full of authority, and feeling his strength. I felt quite calm. Slowly the bandages were unwound. I couldn't see. I kept whispering to myself: "Let there be light, let there be light." Mercifully my eyes were only temporarily affected, though the left one never got back quite to normal.

I went into the hospital and McIndoe operated on my torn-away lip and my nose, broken in two places, and a large nasty gash between my eyes. I asked him, while he was about it, to remove the knob at the end of my nose, but he refused. He said, "Nothing will induce me to play around with your face, I will only do a repair job; you can always play tragedy on one side of your face and comedy on the other."

McIndoe was a remarkable man. He became famous later during the war, operating and grafting skin onto the smashed faces of pilots shot down in flames and badly burned. But he did much more than remake their faces and hands, he remade *them* and lifted up their spirits and gave them hope for the future and the tremendous courage needed to face life however scarred they were at the end. I met one of the pilots who was on the Dambusters Raid and who had been very badly burned. He, like everyone else, admired McIndoe more than words could express. He said McIndoe had given him back his self-respect and, whatever he looked like, he no longer wanted to hide away.

It took quite a time to recuperate and there were moments when I thought my face would never heal.

But I was back at last in my first important but small role as Leslie Banks' daughter in *Service*. There had been an audition for this part for a girl not over sixteen. My agent had lied about my age, and I had got the part. From then on I felt a certain amount of guilt. In the play I had to carry two dogs, Sealyhams, under my arms on to the stage for my entrance. During one dull matinée, a silly woman in the front row of the stalls leaned forward and said loudly, "Poor little dogs, poor little darlings—never mind, I love you." Then she whistled. Both dogs whipped around and started to growl and yap and kept it up, while the audience woke up and started giggling. My entrance had to be changed as the dogs never forgot. The moment I stepped onto the stage each night they struggled frantically to find the woman, barking their heads off as they searched for her over the footlights. I remember how Jack Hawkins, who played my brother, laughed at my embarrassment.

Plays seem to run much more smoothly nowadays, but I remember many instances of things going wrong in the past and certainly unforeseen dramas during the run of a play. We had another incident in *Service*—a matinée again—when I was playing my one and only important scene with Leslie Banks. He was a big star and I was in great awe of him. I was on my knees, my face hidden in his lap, sobbing my heart out (because in the play he had married again) when Leslie suddenly stood up. I fell flat on my face on the stage. He then strolled down to the footlights and, shading his eyes with his hands, glared ferociously into the audience. Then, with a loud voice, he bellowed at two white-haired ladies sitting in the second row of the stalls, "Ladies—I have had enough—do you hear—of your chatter while I am performing—I suggest it would be a good idea if you leave the theater and discuss your successful shopping spree somewhere else—then we can continue."

There was only a slight pause, then one lady turned to the other and said, "Yes, Maud, that is a good idea, don't you think—shall we go?"

They then proceeded to pick up all their parcels, smiled at us on the stage, said "Thank you" and made their exits.

Leslie stormed back to me, grabbed hold of me, threw me on my knees and said, "Go on," and I started my sobbing again.

Perhaps we haven't the outsize personalities now that existed then, but I don't see a modern actor losing his temper and stopping a play. It was funny, of course, but outrageous behavior. We should always remember that we are "servants of the public," whatever that means, but then Leslie was an outstanding personality with enormous strength and attraction and had a large following.

This reminds me of one more rather hair-raising interruption also at a matinée in the theater: perhaps matinées attract this sort of thing. The play was *Lottie Dundass* at the Vaudeville Theatre, which I will describe later. I was playing my first big star part. The audience was suitably silent and, I hope, enthralled with my performance. You could hear a pin drop. I walked down to the footlights and, with arms outstretched, started a long, moving speech. I had got to about the middle when suddenly I heard a loud male voice from the audience shout, "Ssh—ssh—please be quiet and listen to this great artist."

Astonished, I stopped speaking. In the stalls, standing with his back to the stage, was a man waving his arms about. He began to shout again, "Do you hear what I say? Be quiet."

Furious, I raised my voice to a high pitch and continued my speech, successfully swamping him. There was a scuffle and I presumed the man was removed.

After the play was over I was sitting in my dressing room, taking off my makeup, when there was a knock on the door and before I could answer Robert Newton, the actor, almost fell in.

"My darling," he said, "how disgraceful it was—the audience making all that noise, but I silenced them."

He came over to take me in his arms and received the best double smack across his face that he had ever imagined. To my surprise he fell on his knees on the floor. Dear Bobbie, he was at worst a colorful rogue and greatly enjoyed the good things of life, sometimes through a haze, and he was a great actor.

Whoever starred in a play in those days was of great importance. Now the play, production and director are usually more important. But I feel it is different in the films and television, partly because the audience is more intimate with the personalities concerned. In the past people got very involved with the characters the actors were playing. They wondered what happened to them when the film was over and lived through their problems. The stars were "tailored" to this and given parts that suited their personalities. Things were changed for them in the script sometimes to bring out the best they had to give. I was once asked on a television program what the difference was between a star and a great actor. I think the basic answer is that people go to see a star for the magic of his personality, or maybe looks, not primarily for his part in the play or acting ability, and when the performance is over the audience leaves really caring about him, or her. Any great actor, on the other hand, will have people talking in the bar during the interval: "Isn't he marvelous—a fine performance—how does he do it?" It's as if the audience is sitting back appluading but not all that involved. Of course the exceptions are when an actor has both these attributes, but somehow the cleverness of actors—anyway to me—can be brilliant manipulation and a lot of brainwork, without that extra something. No one could represent a star rather than an actress better than Marilyn Monroe. She had an essence impossible to explain: magic, mystery (most important) and love that she gave out in everything she did. Men and women loved her in return; she somehow demanded it.

It was while playing in *Service* that I met my first husband, Victor Malcolm. He had seen the play once or twice, was introduced to me, then proposed marriage a couple of weeks later. When I said I would like to think it over, he answered, "Oh, why? Much more exciting to get engaged, then think it over, than to think it over, then get engaged." Victor was the grandson of Lillie Langtry. His mother, Lady Malcolm, was the daughter of the famous Jersey Lily—a great beauty of her time and paramour of Edward VII, when he was Prince of Wales.

Before we married I had to be "passed" by my mother-in-law-to-be. I arrived at the Malcoms' house in Onslow Square and was shown up to her boudoir. Jeanne Malcolm was very imposing, but I am told she had not her mother's charm and personality. She was lying on a Récamier sofa covered with a silk shawl. The room seemed a bit dark. She had a headache, and a maid was sprinkling some sort of scent over her. The maid was dismissed.

I stood by the door. Actress or no actress I was still ridiculously shy. Lady Malcolm pointed to a low stool near the sofa, and I sat down on it and gazed up at her. I thought she was very beautiful but seemed to have even more makeup on than I used in the theater in order to be seen by the gallery. The scent in the room was heavy.

I always remember what I was wearing at important moments in life, as if my clothes were there either as friends to enjoy the fun or to protect me. At other times I find them rather a bore. On this day I was wearing a full gray skirt, a short box jacket with a Gigi collar and bow, a small black velvet pillbox hat and, daringly, a little black veil that reached to above my nose and, what I will never forget, short white gloves which worried me terribly as I felt I should take them off—but when?

My mother-in-law-to-be, having looked me up and down and, I presume, with a flash of inner sight, judged me, then said rather startlingly, "Are you a virgin?" If the stool hadn't been so low, I would have fallen off. No one in our family ever mentioned that word—it didn't exist as far as the Todds were concerned. I wondered frantically what she wanted me to answer, at the same time not liking the idea of proclaiming myself a failure. So I took a big breath and said, "I'm afraid I am," and looked appealingly up into her face. My mother-in-law-to-be laughed and from then on we became great friends. I still don't know why she asked me this question or what it had got to do with her anyway.

Jeanne had many stories to tell of her childhood. She told me how her mother and she used to have to dash around the house when they heard that the Prince of Wales was about to call, whip all Lillie Langtry's pictures hurriedly off the wall before he arrived and hang up those that he had given her, which had been taken down.

Victor and I were married at St. Margaret's, Westminster, by the Archbishop of Canterbury, Cosmo Lang. Because His Grace was marrying us, the bride had to arrive before him and so, to get the timing right, Father and I got there early and circled in the car around and around the Cenotaph.

I suddenly put my hand in his and said, "Father, can I come back if it doesn't work out?"

He answered, "Of course, lassie, any time, remember."

The church was full of theater people, friends of the bride and groom, and *Debrett* was much in evidence. I had eight bridesmaids; one was Mary Malcolm, the well-known former television personality, who became my sister-in-law and who, I like to feel, still is after many changes and many years. I have always thought that the Jersey Lily bestowed a bit of herself and her beauty into Mary and perhaps missed out on her mother.

My husband was tall and handsome and he wore the kilt for our wedding. I had a beautiful gold-and-white dress and my great-grandmother's veil over my face. My headdress came from Pacquin in Paris but did not make the success it should have done because they forgot to put in the instructions and I wore it like a halo, when it should have been very chic, tipped forward onto my forehead. My train could have got a laugh. It was nearly three times longer than me. A friend who was in the church said that when I passed down the aisle she thought it would never end; it went on and on, attached to my small figure far away at the altar as if holding me up to the earth.

At the reception afterward at Calridge's, Mother was happier than I had ever seen her—she was radiant. It wasn't a duke—but not bad!

My husband was a great racing man and gambled heavily. I remember after the wedding, when we went to another hotel for me to powder my nose and calm down, how hurt I was to see him reading the back page of the *Evening Standard* for the racing results and ignoring the front page, which was plastered with photographs of his bride. I was really hurt and behaved like a goose.

Victor and I inherited the Langtry racing colors, beige and turquoise hoops, and we raced a horse called Balbo carrying these colors. Balbo was given to us as a wedding present. I used to feel so sad for him; it wasn't his fault that he was neither horse nor pony—too large for one race, too small for another, and always last. When we went to Newmarket to watch them training, I once or twice rode out myself with the "string" on the Downs and watched my poor Balbo coming out of the mist, hours after all the others had arrived, and hearing Ted Leader, the famous jockey and trainer, call out, "What is *that?*" and me whispering back, "That's *ours.*" Balbo was sold later; I can't remember whether as a pony or a horse.

We led a very social and rather hectic life. I was presented at Court, which included sitting in a Rolls Royce in the Mall with three white feathers attached to my head and wearing long white gloves, etc., while the crowds lining the route to Buckingham Palace gaped at us. I felt like a fish in a tank.

We went on short weekend trips to Le Touquet, where Victor gambled through the night and I never knew what to do with myself. We did have one lovely moment when my father-in-law who was Sir Ian Malcolm of Portalloch in Argyllshire, known as the Baron, was asked to take some of the family to Paris, as the French were giving a reception and dinner to the Duke and Duchess of York. We were told we were expected to dance the reels and I was to partner the Duke, who was later to become King George VI (after the abdication of the Duke of Windsor). The Duchess, who is now known as our beloved Queen Mum, danced the reels superbly, and I am sure she still does. Victor, his brother Angus, Mary and I danced with the Duke and Duchess of York to a most appreciative French audience in one of the beautiful rooms at Versailles. The women wore, as is usual, white dresses and the tartan sashes across the shoulders; the men wore their kilts. I did the Royal curtsey, as I had been told, to the Duke to signal the start of the Eightsome Reel. The French were very surprised at the shouts and barbaric noises that the men made, as we do in Scotland, and the way my husband swung the Duchess off her feet. The moment I heard the bagpipes I was in heaven, even when our future King gave me the wrong hand for the chain, which upset the whole formation and everyone thought it was my fault. After the chain was over and I faced the Duke again to "set" to him, my eyes on the ground, he said, "I am so sorry, that was my fault."

My son was born a few years later. At last I felt I had grown up. It had taken a long time. He was very beautiful and, to my joy, though I didn't really believe it, everyone said he looked exactly like me. I called him David. After he was born, about the time of the abdication, the Archbishop paid me a call and said he wanted to see my son—later on he christened him. I will always remember how tired and small the Archbishop looked. He sat very still with his hands over his face. He didn't speak.

Then he said gently, "I have been today to see Her Majesty [Queen Mary] in her great distress. Then I saw the Queen-to-be, who has so many difficult responsibilities ahead. But now I am able to see the happiness of a young mother full of joy and pride in her first child."

It was at this time that I met Cookie. This isn't her real name, which is Diana Cooke, but everyone, even now, knows her as Cookie. Victor and I were at some smart party at Quaglinos when the lights were turned down for the cabaret to begin. Sitting at a table quite near us I saw a girl with the most attractive profile—suddenly she

turned and waved to Victor; we were introduced and thus
began a long and wonderful friendship. Cookie later
became my secretary, friend and confidante. She traveled
abroad with me and stayed by my side through all my
marriages. She has now been secretary for many years to
Anthony Quayle and is well-known in the entertainment
world and loved by all. I still rush to her for advice and
help when needed.

Unfortunately my marriage to Victor didn't last very
long. We were completely incompatible and I got desperate trying to help him out of various crises. I left him and,
after a long delay, he finally divorced me. Before this
happened, I went to see the Archbishop, as I felt I owed
him that because of the publicity he had had when he
married us. Many people have criticized Archbishop
Lang and have called him a hard man, especially over the
abdication. All I can say is that he showed me understanding and love that, up till then, I had not experienced
except from Tanty. I possess many of his letters written to
me at this time, which will be given to Lambeth Palace
after I have died; they show what warmth and compassion he possessed. He became a great friend of mine, and
I was staying at Lambeth, I remember, when His Grace
was asked to support the Euthanasia Bill in the House of
Lords. He asked me to join him in prayer in the Chapel
for guidance and we went there alone.

He had a lovely sense of humor. Once when we were
walking along the cliffs at Dover in a very strong wind,
after driving at breakneck speed from Canterbury, where
I was staying with various other young people, he said:
"My child, it is amusing to think that if we were blown
over the cliff there would be headlines in the papers
tomorrow: 'Archbishop and actress blown over cliff.'"

I used to call him Arch, so I called back over the wind, "No, Arch—'Actress and Archbishop blown over cliff.'"

The Archbishop died many years later at the station on his way to have tea with me and the children in our little house in Chelsea. His housekeeper, Mrs. Opey, telephoned me to give me the news. It was a sad day. I felt his going very much.

CHAPTER 5

"Let Me Live Till I Die"

The day war was declared I was playing in the theater in a play called *The Man in Half Moon Street* with Leslie Banks. Rex Harrison should have appeared as the young man in it but he was much too individual and ahead of his time as an actor to please the director. He got the sack—how foolish they were. The play was a big success and had been running some time. It was a fascinating story of a middle-aged man (Leslie) who has had a very bad accident and has lost his memory and thinks he is still young. While he is in the hospital suffering from amnesia he falls in love with his young nurse (me) and wants her to marry him. He has no recollection of his marriage and when his wife comes to see him he doesn't recognize her. She is a complete stranger. There comes a moment in the play when the doctors give him a mirror and he sees himself as he really is. Leslie was wonderful in this scene. Every night it was so moving that I could hardly bear it. As the nurse I had to stand in the shadow in the background and watch his agony as he realizes what has happened, that in the loss of the missing years he isn't young anymore.

The evening performance on the day war was declared was rather nerve-racking as everyone in London was expecting our first air raid. Thinking that the Germans might attack that night, rather naturally no one was interested in going to the theater. When the curtain went up there were ten brave people "out front." Leslie went on stage and asked them to come down from the gallery, upper circle, dress circle, and pit, and sit in the front row of the orchestra, so that we could all be close together. It was most eerie as all lights that weren't completely necessary had to be extinguished because of the order that London had to be blacked out completely, so after leaving a darkened stage we had to feel our way with flashlights to our dressing rooms. Unfortunately both Leslie and I were gigglers and we seemed to laugh our way that night all through what was a serious play. I expect it was nerves, waiting for the first bomb to drop— which didn't happen—anyway, we raced through the play in double-quick time.

I got into a taxi and drove through the night to Market Drayton in Shropshire to join my small son, Tanty and Nigel Tangye, a friend who later became my husband. He had been called up earlier by the Air Force and was stationed up there. During that long drive I realized how important it is to belong to someone who cares, when one is in danger, and for a woman, how necessary it is to have a man around, even when one is ninety! It was interesting when the raids were on and there was fear for survival; couples who weren't getting on or even disliked each other rushed into each other's arms and clung together rather than be alone.

After my divorce I started to work very hard, apart from anything else to help support my son. I did various plays and films of not much importance.

I don't really consider myself an actress. I don't think I ever act. The parts I have played in my career that have come off best have usually been a continuation of myself. Lady Macbeth, whom I played much later at the Edinburgh Festival and at the Old Vic, was the Celtic wild side within me—even wanting to murder sometimes! Peter Pan felt like me—I seem to want to float through life. There was the mad Lottie in the stage play of *Lottie Dundass*—I feel dangerously mad like her sometimes. And *The Seventh Veil,* even at the time of making the film I was drifting through a sort of mist in my private life, waiting to be released.

Real actors and actresses are those such as Peggy Ashcroft, Dorothy Tutin, Paul Scofield, Tom Conti, Judy Dench, Helen Mirren and Glenda Jackson, among many; people superb in their art who can play any character, which I cannot do unless it is somehow part of me in one way or another.

Later on I played in two important films but only in very small parts. The first in 1938 was *South Riding.* I was Ralph Richardson's mad young wife and had to ride up a staircase side saddle in hunting get-up brandishing a whip, about to beat Ralph over the head in a mad passion. The scene had to be filmed in one take, as both the horse and I would have been too frightened to repeat it. The hooves made a terrible noise on the stairs; furthermore, horses and I don't see eye to eye. In fact, the moment they look at me I start to tremble. The director practically had to beat me instead of the horse to do the scene at all.

The second film was *Vacation from Marriage,* in which I also had a very small part. This starred Robert Donat and Deborah Kerr. I played a nurse, and the great cameraman Périnal photographed me like a mystic angel. The result was that Hollywood made me an enormous offer to leave England and go to America on a seven-year contract. I have never done anything yet just for money, and I considered my son was of course more important, so I turned it down.

In *Vacation from Marriage,* which Alexander Korda directed, I had one very tragic scene to play with Donat. In the film he had fallen in love with me when I was nursing him—a wartime romance. He wanted us to have an affair. I told him that I was in love with my husband and that he was very close to me and I was very, very happy and I couldn't even consider anyone else. Donat said: "I didn't know you were married. Where is he?" And I answered: "Oh, didn't I tell you? He was killed three years ago."

Korda made me play the scene against the words—with a smile—and it was extremely moving. I had several fan letters from people who swore they could see the dead husband as a shadow in the background. Courage, I believe, is one of the most wonderful things in the world if one can possess it, so I was able to play the scene with real conviction.

Korda was a remarkable man. He was one of the last great film impresarios. In his production money seemed to be no object; the curtains in a scene had to be the best velvet, the furniture real antiques. He represented everything I admire; he thought big, had tremendous style and demanded style from all those who worked with him, but I think his greatest quality was his devastating charm. In an argument he could get around anyone, from politicians to artists, and he nearly always won. One felt one could ask his advice about anything. I remember, not long before he died, sitting on the floor of his office eating sandwiches while he was answering numerous telephone calls and, in between, trying to work out my marital problems for me. There are not many people like him now in our profession.

After this I was asked to be in one of my favorite stories, *Peter Pan*. The war was just beginning and playing Peter was like flying away from all the horror and evil into space. I adored the flying, the freedom, the fun of looking down on the mere mortals below. Joyce Redman was Wendy and she was adorable. Alastair Sim played Captain Hook, and I think most people would agree that he was one of the best ever. I loved playing this part so much that sometimes I used to think: "Oh, what the hell, why bother to grow up?"

We had a few funny incidents during the run of the play. At one performance I was sitting on my toadstool playing the pipes when Captain Hook hit my leg instead of the toadstool, so when I was supposed to stay floating in the air, I was suddenly turned upside down. The man who flew me couldn't see what had happened, and I was carried head down at great speed to the end of the pirates' ship to throw the bomb over the side at the crocodile in the water below. At that moment a real bomb dropped outside the Winter Garden Theater and the audience and I lost all count of what was real and what was a fairy tale.

My leg was quite badly bruised so the moment I left the stage my dresser soaked a bandage in ice water and bound it up tightly. There was no time to get my tights off, or the harness one wears under the tunic for the "flying" sequences; so, bandaged from knee to ankle, I hopped back on stage. Over the footlights came a sound like falling autumn leaves—a kind of whispering concern seemed to envelop me. Little voices urgently murmuring "Wassamatter with Peter, Mummy? Wassamatter with

Peter, Mummy?" The sound swelled up into a wave of sudden insecurity until I started to hop about with joy attempting to dance. Then the wave retreated and we all felt happy once again.

After this, the management took us to Aberdeen, my hometown. It was the first time that Aberdeen had shown the play, which is well known as a very difficult one to put on, with many mechanical problems apart from the flying. At the opening performance the scene for the nursery was set not quite correctly. This can be tricky for the flying, also dangerous. I got ready to fly across the stage to the mantelpiece, the most difficult flight in the play. I wiggled my shoulders to give the cue to be lifted and stood on my marks when, to my surprise, instead of going to the mantelpiece, I was wafted up to the roof of the theater to meet a stagehand reading *The Express*, who was equally startled and did nothing. So I descended at a frightening speed back again on the pendulum across the stage, knocking down the unsuspecting Darling family on my way up to the roof the other side, where again the surprise was too much for another gentleman. In the end, to stop me swinging backward and forward forever, they brought down the curtain.

There was another mishap at Blackpool. I called out as we prepared for a dramatic flying exit to music, "John, Michael, Wendy, now to the *Never-Never-Land*." Then we flew straight into the window that should have been open but wasn't, and we landed on our bottoms in a heap, back on the nursery floor.

On another occasion, in the Potteries, when I appealed to the children to save the fairy Tinker Bell's life and they did so—"Thank you, thank you, she is all right now"—I turned to see that Tinker Bell was stone dead; the light had gone out—fused.

One doesn't play *Peter Pan* only to children, of course.

There are the big grownup children as well. At one
performance I noticed a really very large elderly gentleman sitting in the front row of the orchestra. He seemed
to be by himself. Directly behind him was a little girl
bobbing up and down, throwing herself from left to right
as she tried to see around him. So I wrote him a letter
during the interval.

"Dear Fat Man," I said, "Would you mind very much
changing your seat with the young lady behind you? It
would be very kind if you would do this. Thank you. My
love, Peter Pan."

The next time I flew on, the two had changed places,
and he waved and blew a kiss to me.

It is a lovely play, full of deep understanding, and what
magic and what sadness of lost dreams one feels in
Peter's search for love.

When the air raids got bad in London, the manager
used to stop the play, and I would go on stage and make a
little speech. "Mummies and Daddies, aunts, uncles and
friends and children, there is a lot of fighting and noise
going on outside, so I, Peter, suggest you stay safe and
cozy underground with the Lost Boys and me till it's over.
But if you want to leave, now is the time to make your
escape." Very few people left the theater.

The other stage play I was in during the war was *Lottie
Dundass* by Enid Bagnold, a very dramatic psychological
thriller. The great impresario, C. B. Cochran, had sent for
me and offered me the second lead. I dressed myself up
and went for my interview. When I got home I wondered
why I hadn't been offered the lead, so I returned, rather
courageously, I thought, and saw C.B. again. This time I
wore a raincoat and beret, no makeup. He didn't recognize me at first and I said: "Why can't I play Lottie, Mr.
Cochran?" He answered: "Because you are not wild or

passionate; you are more suited to the character of Rose."
I said: "How do you know, Mr. Cochran? Wouldn't it be
more exciting for me to look like Rose with my long
blonde hair but *be* Lottie, because I 'feel' her, Mr.
Cochran? I *am* passionate, wild and strange underneath.
Please believe me." I played Lottie.

Enid Bagnold got the title for the play from a tombstone
in Brighton. It was her first play in the theater and came
after her great success with her novel *National Velvet,*
which was made into a film with Elizabeth Taylor; a few
years ago there was a Bryan Forbes production with
Tatum O'Neal. Lottie Dundass is my favorite part in the
theater, psychologically complex, tremendously dramatic.
On paper the plot may sound over-melodramatic, but in
fact the play was such an unusual and fine production
that the effect on the audience was spell-binding. My part
had everything: comedy, tragedy, madness—and she was
a murderess! What more does an actress desire! It was
my first real star part; Sybil Thorndike played my mother
superbly and helped me to make the success I did.

The play had a further point of interest: the set for most
of the play is a "play within a play." The set therefore was
divided into three parts. The star's dressing room was on
one side with a door into the passage in the middle, which
ran up to the "stage door" at the back and the "street." On
the other side of the passage was a door onto the "wings,"
where an actor stands before making an entrance.
Beyond this could be seen a bit of the "stage" and the
"actor" or "actress's" back view with strong theater lights
on them. The dialogue and applause of "audience" could
be heard faintly in the background—the "play within a
play."

The story was about a strange young girl of twenty
living in Brighton with her family of seven brothers and

sisters (not seen but heard off stage). Lottie was selfish, incapable of real affection and of receiving the kindness and humanity from all around her. Then suddenly like quicksilver she could charm everyone with her radiance. In spite of her unlovable qualities and frightening outbursts of violent temper when she didn't get her way, she was her mother's (Sybil Thorndike) favorite child, partly because she had a weak heart and was therefore spoiled. Lottie had many problems. Her grandfather had been a great actor, but her father following him in the theater was a cheap "ham" actor who went insane, murdered a colleague out of jealousy and was put in Broadmoor Asylum. Lottie believes she has inherited her grandfather's genius and only needs the opportunity to appear on a stage to prove it. Her mother believes that she has inherited creeping insanity from her father.

When the play opens, Lottie is a typist. Then she hears that a small touring company is coming to Brighton to show a well-known play. She is wildly excited as she has read it and actually knows the lines. The day before the play opens the star is taken ill and rushed to hospital, and the understudy who has been given a few days holiday is snowbound and it seems impossible for her to get there in time and take over. Lottie reads this news in the local paper and goes to the theater immediately and pleads with the manager to try *her*. He is desperate, so decides to use her, partly because of the publicity they would get: "unknown girl—amateur—takes over part . . ." The mother is very disturbed because she fears the excitement will affect her daughter's mind. She knows Lottie will be a failure.

Lottie scrapes through two acts of the play then rushes to the star's dressing room to make a quick change of costume and wig. At this moment the audience sees the understudy, covered with snow, running down the passage. She bursts open the door of the dressing room and shouts at Lottie: "I have made it, better late than never. I don't know who you are, but get those clothes off. *Quickly, hurry,* hand them over to me." Lottie stands quite still, stunned, then starts to undress. She stands in her underclothes gazing at the understudy who is chattering away and trying to fix her makeup and wig.

Suddenly Lottie's fury and violence burst out and she attacks her and strangles her with a leather belt. All this time we see and hear the activity going on in the passage and off stage, getting ready for the last act. No one has seen the understudy's arrival, and Lottie drags the body behind a curtain at the back. The call boy bangs on the door as Lottie struggles back into the clothes. "Third act beginners please—Third act beginners." Her mother and friend Rose (Renée Asherson) are in front watching the play, and by Lottie's behavior Mrs. Dundass realizes something terrible has happened. They rush round backstage and are in the dressing room waiting for her when they find the body. The play within the play finishes, and they hear the applause, not, as Lottie thinks, for her acting, but for taking over the part at such short notice. She runs into the dressing room elated as she is now certain she has inherited her grandfather's genius.

Meanwhile, Mrs. Dundass has told the manager to call the police. Before they arrive, Lottie, due to the strain, has one of her periodic heart attacks. Her mother takes her in her arms and refuses to give her the capsule, as Rose entreats her to do, to save her life. Lottie dies in her madness, still dressed as the nun she had played in the last scene of her play.

Sybil Thorndike delivered the last line, *"Gone now,"* so beautifully, as, with a slight smile of happiness on her face at Lottie's release, she rocked her daughter backward and forward at the play's finish. Sybil was such a very great actress and was wonderfully moving in the part of the mother. We performed this play during the Blitz on London; sometimes when the sirens went off and the audience heard Sybil say "gone now," they didn't wait till the end but got up and hurriedly left the theater.

At one performance I remember kneeling at Sybil's feet while she was knitting. I raised my head and found a pool of blood all over the floor—my nose was bleeding—quite badly. Sybil looked at me and said loudly, "Leave the stage, child—plug your nose with cotton wool—put a key down your back and pray. I will wait till you return" and continued knitting.

So, my favorite part in the theater was, without a doubt, Lottie Dundass. After that, Madeleine Smith and Lady Macbeth—all murderesses! I received rave notices as Lottie and was acclaimed as a "Discovery." I think the review I was most proud of was:

> Ann Todd as Lottie proves herself one of the first tragediennes of the younger generation—those who saw her play *Daughters of High Society* in the past will hardly credit her compelling emotional range and star quality.

My answer to this is "because no one bothered to find out." Sometimes it is more exciting to cast *against* the character, and if Cochran hadn't had the courage and taken the plunge, I might have remained a pretty, well dressed lightweight actress forever.

I seemed to be very busy around this time and in 1945 I was in my one and only musical comedy film. I didn't sing and only *just* danced, taught by a most patient

Freddie Carpenter. The rest had to be doubled. I played the chorus girl in *Gaiety George* with Richard Greene playing George Edwardes, the impetuous and brilliant impresario of the gay Edwardian period. He created the famous chorus of gaiety girls originally recruited from the most beautiful girls in the country. In the film part I rose from the chorus, aged twenty, to become the famous George's wife, and ended up middle-aged. It was all very glamorous and great fun. In the beginning I wore: fishnet black tights—high laced boots—a black see-through frou-frou and lace corseted dress reaching to just below the thighs—fringed strapless top and a red curly wig! It was a pity I couldn't sing or dance!

In the war, like lots of other people, apart from acting I was an air raid warden at night. We had a fierce lesbian lady in control of our patrol who shouted at me once in the dark and gave me an awful fright just before an air raid started. "Put that light out immediately," she said. I thought it was a man and called back: "Sorry, sir. I put my flash on to look at my watch." "No excuse," came back the answer. "There has to be complete blackout."

Then a flashlight was shone on my face, and my patrol leader glared at me. "Oh," she said, "it's Todd, is it? Don't let me catch you doing this again, or else . . ."

I was quite relieved when the bombs started coming down. She really had her knife into me for two reasons. One was that I had been given a rather attractive siren suit to wear when tramping the streets in the dark. It was khaki and padded; even the knees of the trousers were padded in case I was knocked over or had to crawl, and it had all sorts of important pockets and a kind of sou'wester which my head and face got lost inside. She was obviously jealous.

The other trouble was when we practiced handling the pumps. It was a Sunday morning, the sun was out. I completely disgraced the patrol as No. 1 on the pump. When they turned the water on, I couldn't hold the hose and got a shock when the water shot out in such force, unfortunately it hit the congregation coming out of church. I was disgraced and demoted on the spot to No. 2.

Nigel Tangye, the author and former BBC air correspondent, and I had met some years earlier and, now that my divorce was over at last, we decided to get married immediately. No one wanted to wait during the war. Nigel was in the Auxiliary Air Force and was called up as a flying officer.

We had a charming little house in Chelsea. At the back we made an air raid shelter. In front we had lots of flowers. One night there was a terrifying air raid on London in our direction. I was alone, as my husband was on duty. Putting a tin hat on my small son and one on myself, I carried him across the backyard as bits of shell fell like rain around us. We jumped down into the underground shelter. I had tried to make the place as comfortable as was humanly possible by painting the walls and covering everything with pictures, but it was very damp and dismal. It was always a wonderful moment when the "all clear" went off and we could crawl out into the dawn, the light and silence, after a night of inferno, hate and destruction.

This night, when David and I had cuddled up on one of the bunks, I suddenly heard Nigel's voice calling me and his well-known whistle. I thought he must be outside the back gate which was locked and that I must let him in immediately. I practically crawled the short distance and above the noise of the gunfire shouted: "One minute, darling," and I unlocked the gate. There was no one there.

Next morning I had a frantic phone call from him. Was I all right? Had we been hit? He had had an agonizing night flying in an American bomber out of London to drop leaflets on Berlin, while the Germans were coming in to bomb London on a lower level. As the American bombers flew out, one of the crew mentioned that they were right over our bit of Chelsea. Nigel said that his wife was below and the man answered: "Christ I am so sorry for you." Then mentally Nigel called out to me and I "picked it up" at the same moment that they flew over our house. We checked the time later. We often had telepathic experiences like this.

Nigel was very good-looking—he still is—and being a writer he is sensitive and artistic. He adored and spoiled me.

During the war our daughter, Francesca, was born in an air raid. Her birth was as dramatic as mine. I was rushed from London when I started my labor pains to a nursing home at Gerrards Cross, where, with other young mothers, I had a bed in the corridor. The nursing home was packed with pregnant women and, when the Germans bombed a wartime engineering factory nearby, this was the moment my Pippin decided to arrive. The lights had all gone out and the doctor had hardly time to take his collar and tie off before she came, in only one hour.

Nigel was away on duty and I was alone. She was delivered by candlelight to a background of bombs falling out of the sky and the doctor's voice saying severely to me: "Please concentrate on creation, Mrs. Tangye, and ignore the destruction around us."

We heard a broadcast by Winston Churchill at that

time to the mothers of England. Some had given their sons for their country and the other young mothers were producing the new generation. When I later met Lady Churchill I told her how much this broadcast had meant to me then.

Francesca was not pretty when she arrived and— maybe because of the bombs and shock—I asked the doctor to put her back! I am glad he didn't, because she turned out to be so beautiful. Both my son and daughter look marvelous, as do my American daughter-in-law, and my French son-in-law, and my three French grand-children, Oliver, Florent, Marie-Maude, and, very close to me, my Scottish grandson, Jamie. I love to have beauty around me, so I am very lucky.

I'm sure I must have seemed self-absorbed and a bit of a bore at times to them all, but perhaps it is difficult for other people to understand that, to create, one sometimes has to be selfish and alone at sudden and most inconvenient moments and, I must add, I always had to work hard to keep things going in the early days.

They all seem happy, which is important, and have made a better success of their marriages than I have.

CHAPTER 6

The Paradine Case

Just as I was reaching stardom in *The Seventh Veil,* the world around me was also changing gears. There had been D-Day with that great mass of ships of every shape and size and the air throbbing with planes setting off for the invasion. It was a curious life we all lived then. Nigel on that famous day flew out in a Spitfire on reconnaissance, taking photos of the effect of the bombing of the night before on the railways, and then he gave me dinner that same evening at the Savoy Hotel.

The following year the war was over. I remember VE Day well. I happened to be at Lillywhite's shopping in the underclothes department when we heard the sirens proclaiming the marvelous news. It seemed as if everyone was playing in a Feydeau farce. We all went mad. People were crying and laughing, and most of the customers in different stages of undress rushed to the windows and flung pants, petticoats, bras and stockings out into Piccadilly. They fluttered down on the crowd below, who had also gone mad, like pink and white colored petals proclaiming our victory over Hitler and turned darkness into light.

From now on we were able to sleep at night in our beds without fear. The most wonderful feeling in the world.

After the success of *The Seventh Veil* I was let out by the Rank Organisation to Hollywood at a great price, and I made a very large sum of money for them.

Hollywood was an experience I wouldn't have missed. In those days, just after the war, "glamor" was the magic word. Everything had to be geared to what the producers thought the public imagined was the perfect romantic male or ideal woman of perfection. If one of your eyebrows didn't match the other it had to be made identical. If your mouth was crooked, that had to be made straight. If you had no bust, they gave you one. Rotten teeth—they whipped them out.

I hasten to say this is what happened in America. We British at that time were only trying to copy and didn't have to comply with these strict rules.

I will never forget the first film I made there. It was *The Paradine Case*. The first day in the studio was a nightmare. They were filming the dinner scene and I was terribly nervous. Alfred Hitchcock, the director, had arranged for the camera to film the whole dinner table, showing everyone present in close-up, all in one shot without cutting. The shot started on Charles Laughton, then moved along to Gregory Peck, Ethel Barrymore, Alida Valli, the Italian star, Charles Coburn, etc., and finally *me*.

"Cut," said the cameraman.

"What's the matter?" asked Hitchcock rather crossly.

"She," he answered, pointing at me, "has a rash and bumps coming up on her neck and chest. I can't film her."

The great Selznick, the producer, looked at his watch; everyone else looked at me. "This pause is costing money, money," they seemed to be saying.

"Take her outside for some fresh air," ordered Hitch.

They walked me up and down to cool my nerves. Back I came and apologized. We started again. It was no good. Again I was banished, this time underground somewhere, and a nurse gave me an injection. I have no idea what it was. When I returned they shot the scene, rash or no rash, regardless. The last thing I heard as, with head bowed, I returned to my dressing room, was someone saying very loudly, "I hope we are not going to have her like that all through the film—good God."

I adored Gregory Peck and fell in love with him. He was always so relaxed, whatever he may have been feeling, and when I was acting with him I learned not to be so tense myself. He used to call me his "bundle from Britain."

Hitch was trying out a new way of shooting scenes in *The Paradine Case*. It was something he was to make a great success of in a film called *Rope*. It consisted of filming sometimes five-minute or longer takes without a break. This was a tremendous strain on everyone— especially the actors. I will never forget the troubles we had with one scene. I was the only person on the screen. I had to enter the front door of my house, call upstairs to Greg, who was playing my husband, take my coat off, kick off my shoes, run upstairs (two floors), enter my sitting room, make a long telephone call, talking nonstop to Greg, who was off screen sitting with his feet up reading his few lines. Then, at the end, when he made his entrance, we had a long and elaborate love scene to play.

We had to film all this thirty-five times! First the front door kept sticking, then there were many difficulties with the camera crane that had to follow me all the way up the stairs, then the trouble for camera, microphone, etc., getting through the doors—either I went too quickly or the camera was too slow, and various people on the set had to crouch on the floor to pull away the furniture as the camera and I passed. Last of all, on the twentieth take, I started to forget my lines and we had to go right back to the beginning again. I think it was a marvelous notion of Hitchcock's because it gave a flow of continuity to the scenes. Unfortunately, it was mechanically very nearly impossible to hold for so long. In the end, Selznick insisted that we should have close-ups inserted in this scene, which defeated the whole idea, as the editor was forced to "cut" into the action to put them in. We had all gone through the agony for nothing.

We had a studio strike in the middle of *The Paradine Case* and all filming was stopped. So Hitchcock and his wife, Alma, asked me to stay for a few days at their house at Santa Cruz. They called for me in that beautiful city, San Francisco, where I was staying with friends, and took me to lunch at the famous Mark Hopkins Hotel. One goes upstairs for drinks, and the bar is always shrouded in darkness to make the view across the bay more startling and mysterious. In 1948 we looked out on Alcatraz Prison, where dangerous convicts were shut up; escape from that island was impossible. I remember the eeriness of it all, as we sat there drinking our cocktails, and I had an uncomfortable feeling of gloating—or shame. Now this is no more, as the prison has been closed.

We were sitting on stools at the bar—Hitch in the middle and Alma and I on either side of him. Hitch turned away from me and started a long and animated conversation with his wife, while I gazed out over the water.

Suddenly I jumped, as someone grabbed my arm and whispered into my ear in a very strong American drawl, "You're a doll—d'you know that? I like your nose."

I turned around. Sitting on the stool on my left was what I considered an extraordinary sight—a very large man clothed from head to boots in white suede, with twinkling silver studs holding it all together and a large gun on his hip. In the hand not gripping me, he held a rather impressive whip with a silver handle. I murmured, "Oh! thank you, thank you," and looked around for Hitch, who was still arguing with Alma.

"What do you do?" inquired the glamorous white cowboy.

As Hitch seemed too occupied at that moment to bother about me, I turned and faced the gentleman and gazed at a most disappointing face. His cheeks were pink like a girl's, and his eyes were extremely small and liquid blue. I didn't need Freud to tell me there was something wrong here!

He dropped his voice and said, "What about eating with me tonight? You're foreign, aren't you? I'll show you the town."

I again looked around for Hitch, but now he had disappeared! I answered, "I am *so* sorry, but I have a date," and looked helplessly around the bar, before spying Hitch and Alma, still arguing, at a table in the corner where we were going to have lunch.

The cowboy said, "Do you know who you were sitting next to just now?"

To his surprise and disappointment I said, "Yes—that's my date."

"Would you believe that!" he drawled. "I hope you get the part, honey. Play it sweet . . . make up to him. He'll fall, and I will be sitting close by, willing it to happen. Courage!"

I left him, and went over to Hitch and Alma. When I told them about my conversation Hitch's eyes crinkled up and his face began to shake (I don't think I ever saw Hitch actually laugh out loud). He then started to act out what my cowboy thought should be happening, giving me a sadistic wicked look as he leered at me! Then he practically went under the table to scrutinize my legs. He kept repeating, rather loudly, "What ex-per-ience have you had, Miss Smith? Can you cry, make love, walk with a swing of your hips on the screen? I will let you know *after* the weekend whether I think you can play this part."

He went on teasing me, thoroughly enjoying himself. I was red in the face and giggling helplessly. Alma was clutching his arm and trying to stop him.

The cowboy had now moved to a table directly behind Hitch. He was staring at me with a "thumbs up" for encouragement and giving me broad grins, as if to say, "You'll make it, honey—you *will* get your chance." Nothing could stop Hitch, who was now acting *and* directing the scene. Then suddenly we realized that my poor sad cowboy had gone—probably to find his horse.

The Selznick studios had showered me with publicity; my face had been everywhere after *The Seventh Veil,* and now *The Paradine Case.* It only goes to show that if the public doesn't read the newspapers, publicity doesn't mean a thing. My cowboy must have had more important things on his mind! But I suppose it was a rewarding experience for a great director . . .

The strike ended and shooting on *The Paradine Case* resumed. I got over my nerves after a while and bravely demanded to see David Selznick—the great Selznick, our producer. I was concerned about the dressing gown that had been designed for me to wear in a scene with Greg, which was to take place in our bedroom as I was getting ready to go to bed. I said, "Mr. Selznick, I can't possibly wear this glamorous brocade garment with a mink collar. It's ridiculous—no one dresses like this when going to bed with her husband."

"That doesn't matter," said Selznick. "The audiences in Arizona and Iowa have got to know you're rich."

"But the 'set' for my bedroom surely shows that I am very, very rich," I answered. "This is a sad and intimate moment in the film. I can't act this scene in *this dressing gown,* Mr. Selznick." Then, getting braver, I said, "You told me you admired the acting and the reality of British films. This won't be real. *Please,* Mr. Selznick?"

"Well, what do you suggest you should wear?" he growled.

"My old Jaeger dressing gown and my sloppy slippers," I answered, and added, "I think Hitch wants me to clean my makeup off during the scene with face cream and a towel. Frankly, to wear brocade and mink would look silly in my eyes and, I would think, the eyes of the audience too."

He gave up. But now that I think of it, I don't remember seeing the shot of me cleaning my face in the finished film. Perhaps that was too much for him, and was cut out.

Selznick had a fascinating idiosyncrasy which I have never found in any other producer. He used to send notes to all departments on his films at the end of the day, criticizing what he had passed (or not passed) in the "rushes" of that day's filming.

For instance, a note to the Makeup Department would read: "Miss Ethel Barrymore's mouth badly made up." To Hairdressing: "Charles Laughton hair very bad will have to reshoot." To Camera Lighting: "Alida Valli beautifully lit—congratulations." To me: "It was worth bringing you 3,000 miles from London. But when filming today, stand up straight. I presume you have a bust—show it."

He was a wonderful man to work for and—like Sir Alexander Korda in England—he demanded perfection always.

I made quite a success in this, my first Hollywood film, thanks to Hitch. Selznick sent me a long, very long cable from America on the night of the première congratulating me. I don't think there are many great producers in the world today who would bother to do this. Of course I still have it, to look at in those stupid low moments in life when a black cloud seems to engulf one and one is *quite* sure one has never achieved anything, ever.

Films in Hollywood in those days were very exacting and from Monday to Friday we seemed to be bought and owned by the producer, no late nights or scandals allowed. One evening the studio arranged for Greg to take me to a première. Our attendance was probably intended to get publicity for our own film. I wasn't used to these great occasions and was feeling very shy. I had nothing suitable to wear, having just arrived from war-weary England, with its clothing ration cards. Loretta Young, the American star, was so concerned about me that she insisted on lending me her white ermine cape. It reached to the ground and I felt terrific. When we arrived at the cinema we had to talk into a microphone to the hundreds of fans outside, who gaped at us as we stood in a blinding light.

Hedda Hopper, the famous gossip writer, introduced me. "And here we have little Ann *Seventh Veil* Todd all the way from England. Oh, she is looking lovely, isn't she? What a beautiful ermine cape, dear."

I had been dumb up to that moment. Suddenly I interrupted her. "Oh, no, it's not *mine*," I said. "It's Loretta Young's. I don't own an ermine cape."

Whereupon, I hardly knew what was happening. Hordes of reporters rushed at me, photographing and asking me questions, and there were headlines in the papers that I was the first actress to say on the radio that I had nothing to wear for a première and Loretta Young had kindly lent me her cape. The later papers declared how clever I had been to attract so much publicity for myself.

I had met Hedda Hopper previously when I arrived in New York before flying to Hollywood. I was warned that she could be dangerous and to be careful what I told her. She took me to dinner at the 21 Club. I was rather overwhelmed by her—she seemed to be just too big, too strong and vibrant to be true. She was famous for her over-decorated hats. The dinner was progressing favorably till she asked me some tricky question about one of my marriages.

"I am sorry, Miss Hopper," I said, "but I would rather not talk about my private life," and I leaned forward and put my elbow on the table to make my refusal more forceful.

Suddenly the sleeve of my lace dress split and my elbow shot out—it was a very big hole.

"Oh, Miss Todd, how dreadful," she said. "How embarrassing for you."

"Please don't be upset, Miss Hopper," I answered. "You see, the dress was originally long and white, but because of our troubles in England during the War, I had the bottom cut off and had it dyed black. It's obviously got tired of the struggle and has at last just given up. Anyway, you now have a good story for your column—"Poverty-stricken British actress's dress falls to pieces on arrival in New York from war-weary England."

She laughed—but she used it!

When *The Paradine Case* was finished, I must confess I couldn't wait to get home, though I had loved working for Hitchcock. He took the trouble to study his actors quite apart from what they were playing, and so he was able to bring hidden things out from them. He always realized how nervous I was and used to wait for the silence before "action" and then tell a naughty, sometimes shocking story that either galvanized me into action or collapsed me into giggles; either way it removed the tension.

The film had taken a long time to make since, apart from everything else, there was a strike in the studio, but Selznick kindly brought Francesca over from England to join Nigel and me to keep me happy. The Americans were most amused when my small daughter announced how sorry she was for them because they had been bombed too. We realized that she had mistaken the new houses being built in California for the rubble and bricks lying around after a raid. New houses weren't much in evidence at that time in England.

Later I returned to America for a television spectacular, *The Snows of Kilimanjaro,* for CBS—a very big and important production. John Frankenheimer directed it brilliantly and it was most exciting. We had an enormous cast. Robert Ryan played the man and I his wife. They kept to the original Hemingway story. It was a big success and won an Emmy.

To hurry things up in those days it was quite usual to have one's measurements sent over from England in advance to Hollywood so that the clothes were practically ready to wear on arrival. This cut down time spent on fittings during rehearsals. But something went extremely wrong over me.

On the first day in the studio I faced Robert Ryan, whom I hadn't met before, in what was meant to be a safari coat and skirt, but they dressed me in an enormous khaki overcoat to above my knees, and a skirt only half an inch longer, encased my thin legs in thick woollen socks and enormous boots (the wardrobe mistress said, without a smile, they were to protect me from snakes!) and topped me off with a solar topee hat down to my nose. They then hung a large gun over my shoulder. I looked incredible. I stood in front of Robert as he lay relaxing in a hammock.

The production manager announced my arrival. Robert raised himself on one elbow, opened his eyes and stared at me. "I don't believe it," he said and sank back into his hammock.

At the last rehearsal before the shooting began when everything was, as usual, in chaos, I looked up at the artificial trees in the studio and saw to my amazement several large live birds hanging upside down, tied to the branches. Whether from nerves or exhaustion, I don't know, but I started to cry and crept into my tent on the set. (I can't bear even flowers wired.) John Frankenheimer was called to come and calm me. John is extremely tall, and I will always remember his crawling into the tent after me, exasperated, I should think, at my behavior, when he had so much to cope with, and saying, "Don't worry, honey, they are OK, each vulture has had a tranquilizer." I presumed this meant that they would wake up when it was time for their performance, but I wished most fervently at that moment that I could be hanging upside down relaxed until I was needed. Soon after this, Mary Astor slipped, carrying a bird in a cage across the studio. She fell and the canary got out and, attracted by the lights around the vultures, it flew straight at them. The vultures, still hanging upside down, dopey with their tranquilizers, snapped at it and missed. The noise was deafening and our nerves were as taut as violin strings.

At last John was persuaded to change the scene, the vultures were untied and fell asleep, and the canary was caught with a butterfly net. I came out of my tent with red eyes and we continued the rehearsal. Robert, more relaxed than us, had slept through all the fuss.

Working in Hollywood with its marvelous weather, smog or no smog, is pretty good, especially the early morning swim before driving to the studios. I usually stay at what was the rather shabby mad Château Marmont Hotel on Sunset Boulevard, and I am always given the suite Greta Garbo used to take.

There are many stories about this hotel. It used to be run by three pixie ladies who sat in the reception desk and who should have been in a film themselves. It was found out that all the keys fitted all the rooms, and if someone was having an intimate relationship and had to keep quiet about it, couples could climb over balconies and drop down a floor. But it was supposed to be a hundred per cent safer to enter the garage in the basement and take the lift from there straight up to the floor to be visited, thus avoiding the disapproving Pixie ladies in the entrance hall. This idea was fine till one day the man who looked after the garage informed someone that he was psychic and always knew exactly where everyone was going. This of course caused some panic and a feeling of anxious insecurity!

CHAPTER 7

"All the World's a Stage"

I never believed I could be spoiled or lose my head, but I was wrong—perhaps I had had too much attention thrown at me too suddenly. Nigel and I began to grow apart. Back in England I was working terribly hard, getting up at 5:30 A.M. to drive to the studios and getting home again late and exhausted. Nigel stayed down in Cornwall with the children in our beautiful house on the edge of the sea and ran our farm. The house had belonged to his parents but I was able to keep it from being sold with some of my *Seventh Veil* contract money, and I went down on the night sleeper for weekends when I could. Nigel found it difficult to get a job, but of course now we had a lot of money. Yet the situation frightened me; I was the only supporter of the family, and I got more and more worried for the future.

Then I met David Lean. David was already a well-known film director and had just made the enormously successful *Brief Encounter*. I was engaged to play in the film *One Woman's Story* based on H. G. Wells' book, with Trevor Howard and Claude Rains, which he was directing. This was my first film after returning from Hollywood. It is usual for the director to meet the stars before starting to work but for some reason David didn't meet me—I think he imagined I would be conceited and grand after the success of *The Paradine Case* and was determined to put me in my place right from the beginning. I was intrigued by the way he ignored me.

We met for the first time in the Albert Hall, where I had been a student and later played the Rachmaninov Concerto for *The Seventh Veil*. At the time, we were filming the fancy dress dance scene in *One Woman's Story*. It was an enormous crowd scene, everyone in fancy dress with balloons and streamers, and so on. I was dancing with Claude Rains, who was playing my husband. David as the director was in the roof of the hall to film the whole scene. Then on "Action," strapped to the camera crane, he swooped down out of the darkness like Jupiter on Leda into a close-up of me. It was sudden, dramatic and possessive—and my introduction to David Lean.

David is a very attractive man—and a superb director, one of the best in the world. I was literally swept off my feet. He certainly wouldn't take "no" for an answer, and I said "yes" in my search for happiness. But it is no good chasing after happiness—like the butterfly it will fly away.

I admired him more than anyone I had ever met. He was married, so we both had to get a divorce. Mine was distressing, bitter and unhappy. Either I wasn't adult enough to cope with the situation, or destiny stepped in—

I don't know—but a love was lost; and, not so important, all my *Seventh Veil* money went in the divorce case. How little material things really matter, though, in the end. Nigel is so happy now and we are great friends.

I married David in 1949 and made three films for him. After *One Woman's Story* came *Madeleine,* the story of the famous Scottish murder case about the Victorian girl Madeleine Smith. Her guilt was never proven in the Scottish courts; the verdict was "non-proven." I had acted in the play earlier in the theater when it was called *The Rest Is Silence.* The Rank Organisation bought the story for me to star in and for David to direct. I possess some of Madeleine's letters to her lover and also the sunshade she carried when in court.

I will never forget the day when we were shooting a scene for *Madeleine* on the beach at Cornwall. I couldn't sleep the night before as I had to face a horse the next morning, which was to run away with me. It should have been quite easy as I only had to play a short scene of dialogue with Norman Wooland. Then, as the horse bolted, they were to stop filming and replace me with a double.

It was a lovely wild day, large waves and a wind; also a big crowd on the beach hoping to enjoy themselves. David was directing from the top of a fast camera car that could follow the horse along the sand.

Trembling like a leaf, I was lifted on to my horse riding sidesaddle with my long skirt draped over my foot and stirrup. Then the focus boy took the tape to measure the distance between me and the camera and shot his arm out across the horse's nose. It immediately stood on its hind legs, pawing the air and neighing. I threw my arms around the pommel and screamed. My hat and veil fell off. David became severe. We started again. The crowd

Myself as a child.

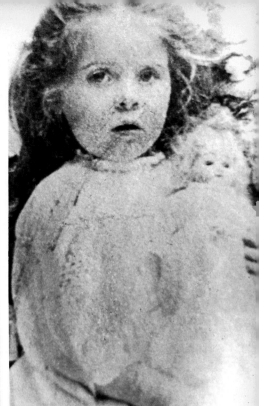

Age fourteen.

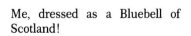

Me, dressed as a Bluebell of Scotland!

With Leslie Banks in *Service*. I was playing his sixteen-year-old daughter.

With Tanty, my beloved aunt, at Brighton.

Nigel Tangye, my husband, taking me for a spin during the war.

Top left, with Robert Donat in *Vacation from Marriage*. *Top right*, as the mad young wife in *South Riding* with Ralph Richardson.

Right, as Lottie Dundass. This was the beginning of the famous hairstyle.

COURTESY DANIEL MAYER AND JACK MIETON

EMBASSY FILMS

EMBASSY FILM

Top left, the "Pin-up Girl" from *Gaiety George*; *Top right*, . . . but I *could* fly! Me as Peter Pan; *Bottom*, "Horses and I don't see eye to eye." A still from *Gaiety George*.

As the child, age fourteen, in *The Seventh Veil*.

Above, with my daughter Francesca at the time of *The Seventh Veil*, near our house in Cornwall.

With James Mason and Whisky at Brighton Beach.

The Seventh Veil.

James Mason and me in *The Seventh Veil.*

The Seventh Veil.

Action still of James Mason hitting me in *The Seventh Veil.*

laughed and I had a nasty feeling my horse was laughing too. "Action," shouted David; then quite suddenly out of the sky swooped down a small open plane. It came straight at us and we all ducked. Flying very low, it skimmed along the beach. Assistant directors clung to the horse and me, seagulls screamed, and the crowd, thinking the plane was part of the film, gazed fascinated and clapped. David lost his temper, clenched his fist and shouted at the plane as it prepared to attack again. On the second run the pilot leaned out and waved to me—it was Nigel! Having successfully stopped all filming, he flew off home, and the director had him reported to the Flying Club. David never knew who it was—I never told him.

The third attempt at the scene was disastrous. The horse didn't wait for anybody; it just galloped away, before the cameras were ready, along the beach nearly out of sight, with me like a sack of potatoes clinging quite desperately to its mane. Then it turned sharply right into the sea, and stopped in surprise when a wave hit it. Norman Wooland, who was hoping one day to play the scene with me, galloped after me and pulled me out. I was really very, very frightened. David was furious with me and also with himself for losing a good shot because he couldn't keep the camera up with the horse. The "double," dressed exactly like me, was ordered to mount—she then trotted back with a happy horse to the starting point to begin all over again, this time without dialogue. Then we heard a voice from the crowd call out, "I don't know what all the fuss is about. They are all mad. They should have used the second girl from the beginning—the other one is no good."

David, a very fine director, never had much consideration for what actors sometimes have to go through—just a relentless drive for what he wanted for the scene!

Last year I was up in Glasgow, and it was arranged for the well-known historian Jack House to show me the actual house where Madeleine Smith had lived with her family, including the cook's room in the basement which she and her French lover took over and where they had their secret love affair for three years. I was fascinated. I was standing in the Smiths' drawing room when I got an electric feeling down my spine and the room lost focus for a moment. I told Mr. House and he said: "Naturally, you were very close to her and both of you are Celts." I wondered if she was trying to tell me whether she *did* do the murder or not—or just letting me know she was there.

The next film I made for David was *Breaking Through the Sound Barrier* with Ralph Richardson and Nigel Patrick. Terence Rattigan had written the part for me, and because of this I found it much more difficult to play and I felt I was being dull. When we have to act as ourselves we sometimes feel rather lost. It is so much easier to be told, "It's a Katharine Hepburn part or a Bette Davis part." But when Terry said, "Nonsense, it's you," I realized how little one truly knows oneself. In the end the part turned out rather successfully and, as usual, I loved being with Ralph who played my father in the film.

Toward the end of the film I had to look nine months pregnant, so a kind of cage was made and strapped onto my body under my skirt and smock. This helped a great deal to give me the heaviness one feels toward the end, the awkwardness of getting up out of a chair and the slightly rolling walk. In one scene in the film I went to the cinema alone to fill in the time of waiting, though expecting the baby's birth at any moment. A great friend of my husband finds me there and breaks the news that my husband has just been killed when his plane crashed coming through the sound barrier. David decided to shoot this scene "verité," as it really would have happened. He had the camera hidden in a workman's hut in the street, in front of a real cinema. I joined the queue waiting to go in to buy our tickets. The public was quite unconscious of what was going on. I wore a scarf over my head and had a shopping bag over my arm; no one recognized me.

When we got up to the box office, the woman in front of me was taking such ages to get her money out of her bag that I received a secret sign from the street to jump in front of her, as the camera was turning. I did this and put my money down for the ticket. The woman whom I had to push out of the way turned on me, red in the face with fury, and shouted, "Wait your turn can't you—what's all the hurry? I was in front of you." Then, with all her force, she jammed her elbow viciously into my ribs. I automatically put my hands over the cage, whereupon the poor woman was horrified. She thought she had killed the baby and, with her arm around me, she escorted me into the cinema murmuring all the time how sorry she was and was I sure I was all right. I graciously told her it had been a shock, but all was well now. I wonder if she ever saw *Breaking Through the Sound Barrier*? I hope if she did she was able to laugh.

Later, David and I were sent as "ambassadors" by the government, traveling to many countries with *Breaking Through the Sound Barrier* to get people interested in the *Comet*, the plane that starred in the film.

When we went to South Africa we stopped off at Entebbe in Uganda. They had made a great effort for our reception. As the *Comet* landed there were banners across the airport (which happened in many places) with "Welcome Ann Todd and David Lean" written in enormous letters. On the pavement stood the black mayoress with an impressive receiving committee surrounding her. I stepped onto Uganda's soil. The mayoress came forward to shake hands, the cameras clicked; she was dressed in the identical gray flannel suit that I was wearing, and the yellow hat and white gloves that went with it! It was a copy, I presumed, of Hardy Amies' original for me. I longed to say, "Snap." Poor love, she was so embarrassed, as if it mattered . . .

We were entertained like royalty everywhere. At one reception in Cape Town a couple of ladies even curtseyed to me! That shows what advance publicity can do!

While we were on this trip in South Africa, we visited a village on one of our long and fascinating drives. Everything seemed golden and looked exactly like the pictures one had seen as a child in books on Africa. When we arrived, the village was full of women, not a man to be seen. David had started to take a film when "the man" arrived in a bit of a fluster. It turned out most of the women belonged to him; he counted them to see that we hadn't removed any. David, to calm him down, asked by signs if he would like a picture taken with me. I might add he was stark naked. He shook his head. David then asked me to have a go. I put my hands together, looked appealingly at him and bowed low from my waist and murmured, "Please? Thank you?" While my head was down, he suddenly raised his voice and said, "Yes, thank you," and as my head came up sharply in utter surprise, he shouted, "and *Bitch*," and bowed with a broad smile on his face, with no teeth. We heard afterward that *bitch* was the greatest compliment I could have been given— meaning roughly, *woman*.

That night we slept in a rondavel in Kruger Park and were kept awake till dawn by two lions that seemed uncomfortably close, roaring at each other, a male and a female. Maybe he was telling her he loved her and calling her his *"bitch."*

What a wonderful working holiday all this could have been, but sadly, I was very unhappy and I think David was too!

Thinking back, I have had very few real holidays in my life. But in 1954 Cookie and I went to Majorca for two weeks. I was about to start up with the Old Vic Company, and I wanted to get myself into shape. Also, more important, to get my voice strong. I used to stand up on the rocks every day facing the sea and shout Shakespeare to the sky. I had never played Shakespeare before, and when I was first offered the parts for the next season I had refused. I felt it might be too difficult for me and that I could never learn the lines. Then someone said: "What a pity, because when you die you won't have Shakespeare mentioned in your obituary in the list of things you have done and that's a shame for a serious actress!" That settled it, and for one year I played Lady Macbeth, Katharina in *The Taming of the Shrew,* the Princess in *Love's Labour's Lost* and Lady Percy in *Henvy IV, Parts I and II.*

It was nerve-racking appearing before those critical audiences and sometimes so exhausting, when all four plays were running consecutively, that one thought it was impossible to continue, but it was one of the most rewarding things I have done in my life. I felt so honored that the Vic thought I could do it.

We used to rehearse from 10 A.M. till 5 or 6 P.M., then rest till we had to make up for the evening performance of another play. We got home at 11:30 P.M., sometimes too tired to eat. There was no social life; we were working much too hard, and that suited me.

I suppose every actor or actress prepares for a part in a different way. Dorothy Tutin, who is a great friend of mine and a marvelous actress, always seems so calm and makes everything look so effortless. She comes to my cottage when she is starting on a new play, and we sit on the terrace facing the sea and discuss it all. I know she is not so calm underneath but goes on striving for perfection even after the play has been running some time. Ingrid Bergman, also a great friend, outwardly appears to be utterly relaxed as well. It always astonishes me how sometimes at an important moment in rehearsal she is able to fly off for some appointment on the other side of the world and return two days later to continue as if there had been no gap. If she ever gets worried about her lines, I always tell her she has only got to stand on the stage and recite the telephone directory; the audience will automoatically love her!

I myself like to have a film or theater script a few months in advance if possible, to be able to study it and "see" myself in the character and work out whatever ideas I have, to be presented to the director later. He is the uncrowned king once we start rehearsing, and one's own ideas of course have to fit in with his concept of the whole. In the theater I find rehearsals the most exciting time of all. One misses all this when filming because, except with top directors or maybe when there is a really tricky scene to work out for the camera, it costs too much money to hold up the shooting. On the other hand, when we actually start filming, I much prever not to know when the cameras are turning. David Lean sometimes used to pretend it was a rehearsal when he was actually shooting on me. The difference this makes to my performance is quite extraordinary, because when it comes to the moment, I still tune in for a second to the old childhood memories and I lose confidence.

In a stage play, on the other hand, I find I can detach myself—sit in the audience as it were—and watch my "other half" and so criticize what she is doing as regards movement, timing, voice, etc. When I played Lady Macbeth, for instance, I "saw" her taking long slow strides and therefore I wore flat shoes for rehearsal. Katharina in *The Taming of the Shrew* had another kind of walk, swinging from the hips and using the heels of her shoes to reveal something important in her character. In costume drama it helps at rehearsal to practice wearing a crinoline skirt, or bustle, to get used to going through doors and to avoid bumping against furniture.

Some actors don't learn any lines of the script till they start rehearsals. They find it better that way. I feel happier learning mine in advance and then ignoring them till we start to work. Noël Coward always insisted that one know the whole part before starting on any of his plays; I feel this certainly helps in films or television, as everything goes so fast one might get into a panic. I don't think it happens now, but in the past, in the big feature films, an actor was known as a "three-take" artist, or a "five-take" artist, etcetera, according to how many takes of a scene were necessary for him to be at his best. I am usually a "three-take" artist; after the third take I begin to go down hill. When David Lean was directing Claude Rains and me in *One Woman's Story*, he always had to decide who was most important in each scene and shoot accordingly. Claude was at his best on take number seven. The director has to work it out. I personally like to work fast—so modern films and television suit me very well.

Nowadays they use hardly any makeup. It's incredible what they used to plaster on our faces. I get really irritated when people think they are paying a compliment by remarking how beautiful we all looked then. I always thought that our faces were like masks and most of the time we looked half dead. I, like others, had more luck, because with my high cheekbones I can look anything that's wanted without a trace of makeup; it just depends on clever lighting. With a light immediately above my head I become a hundred years old; if I carry a candle, perhaps thirty. A side light is the most difficult for the lighting director because of the remaining traces of my car accident, and the coshing that was to come later.

A question often asked is, "You scream, laugh, cry, go mad and die when acting. Don't you find it affects you when you are not playing the part?" The answer is definitely no. If it did, you would be a very bad actress. Just after the performance it takes a little time to disengage, but that is all. The other question is, "Isn't it difficult not to fall in love with the leading actor if you are attracted to each other and playing passionate love scenes?" Again the answer is no, as far as I am concerned. I know we are strange creatures, we actors and actresses, living in a fantasy world of make-believe, but I would find it utterly impossible to be "in love" with a man when both of us were being "something not ourselves," on show, in a blaze of lights in front of hundreds of people. Though, I must add, being "attracted" for the run of the play does help the tedium of playing every night in a long run and should at least keep one on one's toes. I remember one day walking along Piccadilly and running into a very attractive gentleman; I knew him but couldn't remember his name. We chatted and then I said, "Good to see you after so long, where have you been?" He answered, "On a stage with you till three weeks ago." That goes to show how self-centered you can be when acting.

Crying on film or television is sometimes another problem for some people. There are tricks that can be used, but fundamentally it's what you feel inside that matters, not the tears. I think it was Hitchcock who said, "I don't want a close-up of tears pouring down the actress's face, void of all feeling. I don't care if we see her tears or not; the important thing is to see the tears of the audience."

It was usual for my dresser to put out the correct wig for the following night's performance when she left, just to remind me which play we were doing and so avoid a muddle. One night I arrived in my dressing room to see my white wig for the Princess of France in *Love's Labour's Lost* on the stand, so I put on the pink and white makeup, arched eyebrows and rosebud mouth for the part and the beautiful dress, designed for me by Cecil Beaton. It had red and white stripes and a very low neck showing a lot of bosom, and, on top of my white wig, an adorable little golden headdress with bells that tinkled.

I find that, whatever part I am doing, like most actresses I have to get ready early and sit and look at myself for a little while before the play starts, as each makeup is different and you have to feel inside that particular character. On this occasion I was staring at myself in the mirror when I heard, "Overture, beginners, please. Overture, beginners." There was a tap on my door from Paul Rogers, who always chatted to me on his way to the stage. He opened the door and came in. I stopped breathing—he was dressed as Macbeth. I said, "Paul! No—you or me?"

He answered cheerfully as he left me, while the orchestra started up, "You, ducky." With trembling hands the dresser and I tore everything off—my corsets stuck—I jammed on my long red wig for Lady Macbeth, had no time to put her face on (which should have been a green-white base for special lights, false eyelashes and blood red sensual mouth), and was running down the passage as my dresser tried to do up the back of my heavy tapestry dress. I must have looked odd with the delicate pink-and-white face of the Princess surrounded by the rest of my wild Scottish regalia.

I loved our company at the Old Vic, which consisted of, among others, Virginia McKenna, Paul Rogers, Paul Daneman and Eric Porter.

There was a happy atmosphere in the theater that season. Bob, one of the stagehands whom we loved, helped us all and was most understanding with me. For the sleepwalking scene in *Macbeth*, I had to make my entrance, in my long flannel nightdress and carrying the candle, from high up on one side of the stage, down some stairs. My ridiculous nerves used to give me bad cramp every night as I waited in the wings. Bob would massage my legs and lecture me on relaxation and tell me that cramp was the result of bad thinking.

I played the sleepwalking scene differently from how it had been played before, due to a dream I had had. I dreamed that when Lady Macbeth in her madness said, "Come, come—come, come, give me your hand. What's done cannot be undone," she leaned over the footlights and searched for Macbeth out in the darkness of the theater and played this scene as if she saw him and was trying to draw him over to her; so when she then said, "To bed, to bed, to bed," it became in her mind a sensual love scene with Macbeth, and she was smiling. It was only because Michael Redgrave was so enthusiastic when I told him of the dream and gave me courage that the scene was played like this, I think for the first time. I always felt a strange power when playing Lady Macbeth, as if I was dominating not only the theater but the whole world and was somehow awaiting a challenge to this power.

Later the company took the production to Dublin. It was there that I had the really astonishing experience, for the first and only time in my life, of seeming to "leave my body." I felt as though I was being lifted up and was floating a few feet above the stage. I had just started on the "Come you spirits" speech and was able to look down and see myself continuing the performance. Then I looked at the audience and was rather impressed by their concentration as they gazed at my "other self" below. I also thought I wasn't doing too badly! Then, after a few seconds, I seemed to snap back and become one again. It was like returning on a taut piece of elastic. Some people, I believe, have learned to bring about this experience at will. But for me it was quite accidental and, funnily enough, it did not worry me at all, although I must say I am not all that keen on its happening again.

We played *Macbeth* at the Edinburgh Festival at the Assembly Hall on an open stage, which was very frightening till I got used to it, and then I loved it. We had one spectacular scene when Macbeth and I walked through the audience to mount the stage and sit on our thrones. Macbeth, wearing his crown and robes, walked down one aisle with his thanes following him. I walked down another aisle with my ladies following me. I had my crown on above my red wig, and I wore a long purple and gold cloak. The bagpipes were playing and the drums, and the people in the audience as usual were excited and turning in their seats to watch the procession advancing—all except a little old lady sitting next to the aisle. She took no notice of us at all, but as I passed her she suddenly shot out her hand and tugged my cloak. I had to stop and my ladies in waiting, not expecting this, ran into me from behind.

The little old lady looked up at me and said: "How's your mother?" She was a Scottish aunt, and she was not the slightest bit impressed at what was going on. Short of standing in the aisle and having a long chat, there was nothing I could do so I hurried on, running the last bit to catch up with Macbeth who had reached his throne before me.

During my year at the Old Vic, life gave me a few knocks. I think it was only the extremely hard work and exhausting days and nights that got one through. I was also living alone for the first time in my life and had no one to cry to.

The last experience I lived through seemed at the time like the end of the world. It happened during the run of *Love's Labour's Lost.* We had a dress rehearsal for *The Taming of the Shrew* during the day and were playing *Love's Labour's* that evening. I had gone to the theater early and had asked Cookie, who was still my secretary, to ring Tanty and arrange a ticket for her for the first night of *The Shrew* that week—Tanty never missed my first nights if possible. She would come alone by car, and the theater made a great fuss of her. She was always given a glass of wine during the interval, and we also arranged a hot water bottle to keep her warm. She was now near the end of her eighties and—though she never bothered about age and used to say "Don't remind me of it, it holds me back from all the things I still have to do—ignore it— tear up birthday cards after forty"—she *did* hope she might reach ninety!

Cookie rang her up as I had asked, but after two sentences she heard the telephone fall, and silence. She rushed over and found that Tanty had had a stroke. She thought it best to keep the news from me till after the dress rehearsal but had to let me know before the evening performance.

It is an unwritten rule in the theater that actors and actresses go through with a performance whatever has happened in their private lives. I played the Princess in a daze. *Love's Labour's Lost* was Shakespeare's first play, written when he was young, and it's thought he might have experienced, for the first time, the death of a friend. In the play there is a very moving scene when a messenger dressed in black enters, while all the court are laughing and happy, and announces to the Princess the death of her father, the king:

Marcade (a Lord of France): "I am sorry, madam, for the news I bring
    Is heavy in my tongue—The King—your Father—
    . . .
    [He can't finish]
Princess (after a long pause—crossing to him—in a whisper):
    "Dead . . ."
He nods his head—and the members of the court rise and curtsey to her.

I couldn't say it. My lips were trembling too much. I stood rooted to the spot. Everyone waited on stage, then Virginia McKenna who played Rosaline crossed over to me, put her arm around my waist and gave me the strength to continue.

The moment the curtain came down I tore off my clothes and, with my makeup still on, rushed into a waiting taxi. I *knew* she would wait for me. I *knew* she wouldn't go until I arrived and I was right. The doctor said: "Try to make her smile—she hasn't moved. I don't think there is any hope."

I looked at her. She had a wonderful light around her head—what some people call an aura. She looked beautiful.

Why do people think if you are unconscious you can't pick up what is said? How do they know?

I went over to the bed and said quietly: "Hallo, Tanty. It's Kitten. I've made it, darling." She opened her eyes and smiled at me. I asked if everyone would leave the room, except for the nurse, and I lay on the bed beside her, very close, and whispered in her ear about her journey and how I envied her—just as we arranged we would do when the time came. She died in my arms. I left the room and wouldn't go back but sat on the bed in Jane the cook's room, and tried to visualize where Tanty was— but the light had gone out and it was too dark to see.

A priest was murmuring some prayers, the family were gathered around her bed. They tried to make me join them, but Tanty was gone—in her joy, how dare I make her sad—so in the dawn I walked home to my house. I put the key in the door. Whisky, my dog, was waiting on the mat, his head back, howling. He knew, of course. He loved her too.

CHAPTER 8

"For What Is It to Die?"

After the season at the Old Vic, I went to New York to play in *Edward My Son* on TV with Robert Morley, who wrote the play, which I think was one of his best. I had an actress's dream of a part. It was a great challenge for me because the character started very young and ended up old and drunk. I love playing in the New York theater to American audiences. One can feel their appreciation wafting over the footlights if they like the play and performer. They are the most generous audience. One of the plays I was in over there was called *The Four Winds*, written by Tommy Phipps, Joyce Grenfell's brother. My role was a glamorous, very rich heiress, married many times. It was written around the life of Barbara Hutton. It was a rather sad part, showing how she was made use of by the sycophants who surrounded her. They dressed me in the most spectacular clothes and jewels; one of my

evening dresses of white chiffon used to get a round of
applause to itself when I entered. I played a delicious
drunk scene in this dress with Peter Cookson and always
felt extremely happy wearing it. Robert Hardy, who had
been at the Old Vic with me, played the young man in
love with the heiress. He sees her as a goddess to be
worshipped and not the drunkard living on drugs that she
really was.

I don't know what it's like now, but at that time, in
1957, Americans acted differently from us, with quite a
different rhythm. When Bob Hardy and I arrived in New
York, the only English people in the cast, we seemed to
throw off this rhythm, as English actors use more pauses
and a lot of acting between the lines, giving a much more
natural effect. I think when they got used to us they were
rather impressed.

I was sitting alone after it was over on the first night,
feeling a bit lost and an utter failure and extremely
exhausted. My head was on my arms and I was crying,
when the door opened. I didn't look up, then I felt my
head pressed against someone's body and a hand was
stroking it. A woman's voice said, "I understand, I
understand, dear Miss Todd, cry it out. You were magnificent."

I had never met her but it was that great American
actress, Katharine Cornell. I have never forgotten her
kindness and the uplift she gave me.

It was when I was in New York another time acting in
a television play with Wendell Corey called *Black Wings*
that I received a cable from George More O'Ferrall of
student days at the Albert Hall—he was by then a famous
director—asking me to come home and play in his
television production of *La Dame aux Camélias,* and
strict instructions not to look at Garbo's performance as,

he wanted *my* interpretation. I promptly asked the studios to run a copy of *Camille* for me. The driver of my taxi was a fat little Jew from the Bronx. He chatted away, then said, "Are you a foreigner?" I said yes, I supposed I was. He said, "I had a foreigner in my cab last week, looked a bit like you." It was Garbo. The nearest I have ever got to her! No one likes being told they look like someone else, but nothing makes me happier or feel more honored than when this is said to me. In fact I was thrilled after *The Seventh Veil* when the press in America and England mentioned this fact and France dubbed me *"La petite Garbo."* I told my driver I was about to see one of her films. He asked if he could come too, so he parked his yellow cab and we sat side by side in the empty cinema. I had a notebook to make notes but soon gave up, as Garbo's personality held me spellbound. When it was finished, I put my hands over my face and said, "I can't do it, I can't do it." The taxi driver leaned over and patted my knee and in a voice full of compassion and understanding said, "Never mind, love, never mind, you can do other things."

Things had taken rather an unhappy turn for me at this time. David and I had grown apart and were not seeing each other. He was abroad most of the time, and I began to feel rather lost—once again that old pattern of rejection in my life. He was away filming in India when one day I received a telephone call from Ingrid Bergman from Paris to ask if I could arrange an interview with Prime Minister Nehru, who was visiting London and whom I knew.

Ingrid and I have been close friends for thirty years. Our lives seemed to run through the same kind of problems. At that time she was married to Roberto Rossellini and it turned out that he had got into some sort of trouble while filming in India. As a result his film had been confiscated and he was prevented from leaving the country. Roberto had appealed to Ingrid for help. Madame Pandit Nehru, Nehru's sister, who was high commissioner in London, said she would arrange a dinner for us all to meet. Nan Pandit was a great friend of mine; I will always remember how she loved my dog, Whisky. One day when I was visiting her at the Embassy, she was standing at the top of the red-carpeted stairs in a blue-and-gold sari. When she saw us she ran like a girl down the stairs, went on her knees with perfect grace, put her hands together and did the *namaste* to Whisky, who was enough of a gentleman to sit up and beg. He adored her—but then he loved all lovely ladies.

When Ingrid and I finally set out for dinner with Nehru, we took what turned out to be the slowest taxi in London and were most surprised to find about twenty reporters lurking around the corner. They chased us in fast cars all the way to the Embassy, chanting as they went, "What are you two girls up to? Why are you going to see the prime minister?" How did they find out? It always amazes me.

After dinner we had a long talk with Nehru, who promised to straighten things out. Then Ingrid and I came back to my house, again chased by the press. It was a very hot night, and we took off our dresses and had a joyous evening sitting in my garden toasting ourselves with large whiskies and congratulating ourselves on pulling off such a coup!

Later, when all was satisfactorily settled, I received a cable of thanks from Roberto for having arrnaged it all.

Ingrid and I had met for the first time in Rome. She was getting very bad world press at the time about her romance with Roberto and the birth of their son. I felt so terribly sorry for her that I rang her up and asked if she would like to meet me for a chat. She said yes immediately, and we had lunch at a small Italian restaurant at the foot of the Piazza di Spagna and became the great friends that we are.

I often used to stay at the house she and Roberto had by the sea at Santa Marinella in Italy. The train practically ran through the garden and seemed to nearly topple over as it went by when the guard got all the passengers to one side to gaze at Ingrid lying in a swimsuit with the children falling all over her.

Once a fan brought a sheep as a gift for her; they had walked all the way from Sweden. The poor sheep arrived quite exhausted, but, typically, Ingrid settled it in with the dogs of the household and it soon thought it *was* a dog. It was called Meeerde! She is an endearingly natural person and enjoys informal and simple things as I do. Perhaps this is why our friendship has been so enduring. We neither of us are what might be called "actressy" actresses and can be completely ourselves in each other's company.

Ingrid has the good Swedish habit of wanting to scrub and clean everything her eyes rest on. I went to her Paris house once when her staff was away and we put aprons on and got down to it—and she still tries to tidy me up even now when she stays with me in London and in my cottage.

When we are alone together there is nothing we enjoy more than to take our shoes off, put our dinner trays on our knees and watch television and talk about the performances and argue about the plays. I admire my friend very much, in particular because the word courage truly belongs to her, and, as I said before, I value that more than anything in the world.

*   *   *

David continued to stay away, and things got difficult with the press, which made life rather complicated and impossible for me and the children. However, I made one or two films, *Time Without Pity* for Joe Losey with Michael Redgrave, and *The Green Scarf* again with Michael, directed by my old friend George More O'Ferrall.

Then in 1954 David and I parted for good, with a divorce three years later. It left me with a feeling of utter failure in life—I felt passionately that we should have made it work. I decided to get right away for a bit to Switzerland and went there for a climbing holiday with a friend.

Fire plays an important part in my life. First of all, I was born in a fire; then, one day when I was flying in a small private plane piloted by my second husband, Nigel Tangye, the plane caught fire. Nigel managed a brilliant forced landing in a field, and he and his brother Colin threw me clear as the plane burst into flames.

Coming back from this holiday in Switzerland, I was very tired and had fallen asleep. Suddenly I woke up to see an orderly queue forming in the center gangway of the plane and out of my window I could see flames slowly and determinedly crawling along the wing toward us. It was fascinating how calm everyone was. That's one thing the British can really be proud of! Then a "foreigner" shouted: "Why the hell don't we smash the window so that we can get out if necessary." A voice shouted back: "Shut up and sit down." We started to come down to land and below us were ambulances and fire engines all lined up on the pavement. I felt a strange floating sensation as if someone had just removed my mind but, strangely enough, safe. The stewards and stewardesses, immaculate as usual and with calm bedside voices, asked us most politely to get into line for the chute.

The plane came in to land at a frightening speed but got down safely. The lady in front of me was an extremely fat Italian, and when she got to the middle of the chute she became very frightened and started to push her arms and legs out in all directions, then stuck. Someone produced a pole and gave her a shove—she shot down, shouting all the way. I followed in the vacuum of her exit and went down like a streak of lightning. At the bottom of the chute two strapping gentlemen caught me and one said: "She knew, she knew, she wore her trousers! The rest of them arrived on the ground with their skirts over their heads." We all laughed—though mine was rather forced.

We had to leave everything behind in the plane and it was pathetic how some of the women cried out and pleaded for their handbags after we were safe, as if London Airport had taken away their very wombs.

I was asked afterward by the press at the airport what I felt like at the moment of truth. I never know what that means and anyway I was shaking like a leaf. I answered: "Oh, I didn't worry at all. I just thought, 'Lucky people to be traveling with me as I have so much still to do in life.'" I meant it as a joke. It looked terrible though, quoted afterward in the newspapers. What conceit.

Some people have a lot of suffering all through their lives. I am one of the lucky ones—mine came like one big blow, all at the same time. It's hard to believe the Job-like troubles that hit me all within a couple of years. This part of my life must have been arranged far back in time, I think. For some reason there was physical suffering, mental fear and spiritual bewilderment. I seemed to be living in a closed world with no light. It was obviously a battle I had to fight out myself, and win. It is interesting that at important moments in my life, either in joy or suffering, I am always alone. There are no complaints; it seems right somehow.

Before the troubles started I had been traveling quite a lot and televising here and in America. Then ten days' holiday in Greece, on the island of Hydra. As a Scot I love wild winds and storms but I also feel utter joy and fulfillment at home when stretched out under a scorching sun. I once had a long and intense conversation with Judy Garland in Hollywood on this subject. It was about the importance of where one is born and where one feels one belongs. She told me she was certain she shouldn't have been born in America. The vibrations and speed there were much too quick for her and that's why she started taking drugs. She ought, she felt, to have been born in England and I think her life would have been very different if this had been so. Everybody loved Judy. I can see her now, entering my house in London in an old leather jacket, bringing love with her. She was such a warm person. I will never forget going to a party that Dirk Bogarde gave. Judy and I sat on the top of the piano. She had her arm tight around my waist as she sang Noël Coward's songs while Noël played the piano and accompanied her. Her voice seemed to vibrate through my body and, though we were all happy and having a wonderful time, I felt very moved and somehow anxious for her she seemed so vulnerable.

Soon after this I became extremely ill. I had been having bouts of pain for some time, occasionally holding up rehearsals. Then it all blew up and I was rushed into a nursing home and operated on, most successfully as it turned out, but only after many complications and a very great deal of pain. In fact, I learned a lot about pain at that time. I learned, for instance, that if you can accept it and "go with it" and not resist, it's much easier to bear. The operation was at Easter, which seemed as it should be, and Cookie was able to be with me. She bought a cheap Medici print and hung it to the wall facing my bed. I have still got it as a memento of a "battle." The picture was of my favorite elements, wind and sea. The room in the nursing home was very small, because of expense, and I had to be there rather a long time but, by gazing at this picture I could go through into a reality beyond, and the room somehow became bigger.

During the "battle" I died. Then the doctors dragged me back against my will. Carl Jung said, when he had the same sort of experience, "I felt violent resistance to my doctor because he had brought me back to life." Why are we frightened of dying? It is so wonderful. I wish I had the words to describe it to you. What I say sounds trite and dramatic, yet if there is anything that we call truth, this is it. I was holding Cookie's hand and complaining that the air had gone and could the nurse open the window wide, and why was the light fading, and would Cookie read a little bit of the Song of Solomon, "Arise my Love and come away." My guardian angel heard me. He took my hand and I went. Then I had the same experience that I had had as a child, when the lights danced and shimmered and came alive in the church. This time the fruit by my bed was encircled by light. The flowers were the same, alive and seeming to talk, and we were all one; even the sheet when I touched it seemed to be alive and shining. Then it was as if we were in a lift, shooting upward to a dazzling white light. It was unbelievably beautiful when we arrived—the light and music and such brilliant colors, flowers and trees. Ours on earth just seem a bad copy; and there was Tanty, her arms out to me, laughing at my surprise at seeing her.

At that moment I was pulled back into the darkness, back again to earth. Far away I heard someone say, "Thank God, we have got her back."

"Thank God?" I thought. "After seeing a glint of heaven?"

Of course there are those who declare that all this is hallucination or the result of pain-killing drugs, but they are talking about something they have never gone through themselves, about a state that has nothing to do with earthly conditions. The short time I was "there," I can only say that I think I came face to face for one moment with the essence of Love and the pain of too much tenderness. Many people have experienced what I did, but what is important is that nowadays one is able to talk more openly about such things. There should be no fear about death, for there are no such things as live people and dead people. It's so simple, just opening a door, saying goodbye for a little while and going through to what is only a continuation of this life. In fact it takes many people a little time to realize they have left the earth's plane; it is all so natural. Everyone has a "guide" to take them over when they go. No one is ever alone.

My guide is my guardian angel—I continue calling him this just as I did as a child, so long ago. Whether we know it, ignore it, or don't care, they are there to help us on the way. Goethe's last words, said in joy, were, "Light, more light." This note of joy is the sign of the new Aquarian age. As Khalil Gibran tells in *The Prophet:*

> For what is it to die but to stand naked in the
>   wind and to melt into the sun?

And what is it to cease breathing but to free
    the breath from its restless tides, that it may rise
    and expand and seek God unencumbered?

Only when you drink from the river of silence
    shall you indeed sing

And when you have reached the mountain top,
    then you shall begin to climb.

And when the Earth shall claim your limbs, then
    shall you truly dance.

After what can only be called this wonderful moment, things began to change slowly. I had thought that the strange experiences I had had as a child would fade away but they didn't. They remained and just took another form. I began to realize as the pattern unfolded that there was perhaps a reason for it all and that I must now try and learn to understand.

CHAPTER 9

"The Slings and Arrows of Outrageous Fortune"

After David Lean and I parted, I continued to live in our large house in Kensington with Whisky, my dog. Whisky was a tough, sensitive, psychic Sealyham, who bossed me, and we adored each other with an undying love.

Apart from Whisky, there was Mrs. Perkins, known to everyone as Mrs. P., who cooked and looked after me. I don't know, this first time alone, how I could have existed without her.

It was in 1958, and I was playing at the Apollo Theatre in *Duel of Angels*, with Vivien Leigh. We played the two angels, and Jean-Louis Barrault, the French director, came over from Paris to direct it—and what a director! It was like being poured into a poem, being directed by him. A wonderful experience.

Some directors know how to bring out the best in an

actor or actress—even finding things that they themselves don't know they have in them. *Duel of Angels* was a translation from the French play *Pour Lucrèce* by Giraudoux. It had been performed in Paris with the well-known French actress Madame Madeleine Renaud, wife of Jean-Louis Barrault, playing the part of Lucile—the part I played in London after Claire Bloom had given up the role. The play was allegorical and in the costume of the "bustle period," and the dialogue was stylized and beautiful to speak. The two angels, Vivien and I, were dressed exactly alike down to the smallest detail, except as I was depicting "Virtue," my dress, hat and sunshade were all white and I wore a pale blonde wig. Vivien, as the wicked side of the coin, was dressed in black with a black wig. Our director insisted we both must get our waists down to seventeen inches by wearing corsets and suffering agony, all because his wife, who was rather older than us, had managed to do it in Paris.

I am afraid the *Duel* turned into a reality and a nightmare for me. Most of London came to see the "battle" on stage between the two angels, because they had heard the rumors that were going the rounds. Vivien was ill, spoiled and sometimes hysterical with jealousy. It was sad because she had no reason to be, with her outstanding beauty. Though we had been great friends before the play, she took a hate against me and the character I was playing. If it hadn't been for Cookie's help and understanding of the situation, I don't think I could have got through it. As it was, I dreaded going to the theater each night, never knowing what was going to happen next, on or off the stage; or even whether Vivien had decided not to play at all that night.

Sometimes she could be so charming. I had known her for many years before this play, when she was married to

Laurence Olivier, but when she had these moods she could be very unkind and sometimes spiteful. I remember a very small and unnecessary moment when she and I gave a goodbye party on the stage for the last night of *Duel of Angels*. She sent a message to me—"Don't dress up, I won't, it would look too grand—just wear anything, as if at rehearsal."

When I arrived for the party, she was receiving like a hostess dressed in a kind of balldress and wearing her jewels. Everyone else was in full evening dress and the men in black tie. I was wearing a short tweed skirt and a fisherman's sweater.

I did not apologize to anyone and just tried to ignore the whole situation—even her remark to me as I walked on the stage: "Didn't you bother?" she said. "How rude." And she turned her back.

Poor Vivien. Of course if I had known as much then as I do now, I think I could have helped. Because one must learn to *look* at people *within* in a different way than the way people are seen outwardly. Then it can be quite a surprise and things are made clear. But I didn't know this then.

To show how a scene can be changed from something ordinary to genius by a superb director: as Lucile, I had a line . . . "I thirst." I played it with my head back and eyes shut as a statement. A top director always tries to avoid giving an artist intonation but will try to describe what he wants in a roundabout way so that the actor understands without copying. Jean-Louis stopped the rehearsal and came over to me: he used to call me *mon bébé*. He said, "Forgive me, *mon bébé*, but please try again this line with your eyes open wide, and looking straight up into the gallery as high as possible and in a whisper, and using an upward inflection of innocence and questioning surprise, say, "I thirst?" It is almost impossible to write this, but playing it this way gave a new meaning to the whole scene; just that little change was the most brilliant piece of direction—but that's what acting is all about. *Duel of Angels* was a very big success and had a long run.

Our stage door keeper at the Apollo was a wonderful character. He was small and spry and called Alf. He had been a jockey to the Kaiser, played in a circus and done many other jobs and then, when all this got too much for him, he became a stage door keeper. He used to call me Toddy-Ducks! Once when we were having a difficult time with Vivien, he came to my dressing room while I was making up, took my little cross which was hanging on the lampshade and hung it on a nail between her dressing room and mine. Then, with an embarrassed grin he said, "It will all be OK now, Toddy-Ducks."

During the run of the play he became very ill and had to go to the hospital. He didn't know it but he had cancer. They operated but it was too late. I used to go and see him in the men's ward at St. Mary's twice a week after the performance. He would always be entertaining everyone with his racing and gambling stories but one evening he was very bad and in a lot of pain. He asked me to touch his back where the pain was. As I did so, I felt a shiver go right through me like a mild electric shock. I had the strongest feeling—a sort of presentiment—that somewhere, sometime in the past, Alf had had to die in order to save *my* life.

As I left the hospital the nurse said they didn't think he would last the night. I asked her if she could telephone me when it was nearing the end so that I could think about him. I never really expected her to do this, but at 6:15 A.M. she did so and told me Alf was quite out of control and then she laughed. He seemed to have completely recovered; he was sitting up in bed singing, had eaten a meal, had a bath and was boring the rest of the ward relating terrible jokes and wearing everyone out. Later I rang the surgeon; he said, "Yes, it seemed like a miracle," but they were doing another exploration on Friday. On Friday they cut Alf open again and found nothing. I believe in spiritual healing, as many doctors do nowadays. I have always wondered if my touch was used to heal Alf in return for his having saved my life in another incarnation.

Alf lived on, full of life, for another four years, and we used to lunch together at the pub near the theater once a month if possible. He liked to wear his hat at a jaunty angle all through the meal. Then one day he said, "Toddy-Ducks, I think I soon will be off—can you arnenge to be there to see me go?" Timing in life, when it's important, always seems to work out beautifully—I was there. Alf's wife, who became a great friend of mine, and I, sat by her husband's bedside in the hospital and discussed recipes, I remember, as Alf slept. Just before he went he said, "Toddy-Ducks, why is Mildred my sister here? And old George, haven't seen him for years. What's he doing? I thought he was dead. Good to see you, George." Alf saw them all waiting to escort him, and his exit was full of joy.

Just about then the daughter of Mrs. P., my housekeeper, was going to get married and we arranged that she should have the reception in my house after the wedding. There was room to put up some of her friends and family afterward. I decided to go away after the Saturday evening performance to give Mrs. P. complete freedom of the house for the wedding, so Whisky and I went off to Brighton for the weekend with Cookie.

We arrived late at the hotel, about midnight. Cookie went to our room with the luggage, and Whisky and I went down the road for him to widdle, before going to bed. There was a full moon and I could hear the sound of the waves on the beach and the drag back of the sea across the pebbles.

No one was on the front at that hour except two young men standing very still, like wax figures, on the corner. They were looking at us. Whisky and I started to return to the hotel when suddenly for no reason I wanted to run. At that precise moment they rushed at me and attacked me. I don't remember much except the sudden fierce pain on the left side of my head and face. Then I lost consciousness.

Actually one man had cut my head with a cosh and the other had damaged my jaw with a knuckle duster. I don't know how long I lay unconscious on the pavement. The doctor thought it might have been about ten minutes. I remember afterward thinking how funny I must have looked, sprawled out under the moon and no one but the moon to care. When I regained consciousness I was still lying there alone. Whisky was walking around and around me in circles, making pathetic moaning noises. I wondered why he was covered in blood. I didn't realize then that it was my blood.

I got on my knees but couldn't stand up. I then tried to shout, but nothing came out. I tried again to get to my feet, but it was impossible and my back hurt badly. So I decided to crawl along the pavement toward the hotel. If I ever had to play a scene similar to this in a film or television I can tell you it wouldn't be like what we see usually on the screen. This was ugly and degrading; I crawled painfully forward, inch by inch, my overcoat flopping around me, my handbag gone, and a shoe lost.

Many people are beaten up in our world today, but twenty years ago it didn't happen very often. I wonder if others who ave had this experience felt as I did. It was like a cloud of shame enveloping everything, shame that two human beings could actually smash up another human being—a stranger—for a few shillings and a petty feeling of power.

In the many nightmares I had after this, I would wake up shouting, "Why did they have to hate me so?"

After what seemed a lifetime I was found by a fatherly policeman who carried me into the hotel and held me firmly in his arms, soothing me until the ambulance came. No one recognized me as my face was so swollen and bruised, until Cookie arrived on the scene. In the hospital they found out I had been kicked down my spine, they presumed after I was unconscious. This made it painful to be either on my back or on my face in bed.

Charles Laughton happened to be staying in the hotel at the time and I was so grateful to him for being concerned about Whisky. He gathered him up and took him to the kitchen and fed him on sausages to try to stop his trembling. Thank God they didn't touch him when they attacked me, though he got a bad press the next day for not defending me! The two men were later caught and given two-year prison sentences. I had to go to court to give evidence with my face covered by a veil.

I received a letter afterward from the gang the men belonged to in London, saying that they were sorry when they found out that it was me, as they enjoyed my performances in films and on television. That made me furious. I presume they wouldn't have worried if I had been some unknown old lady they had blinded.

Cookie was able to persuade the doctor to allow me to be driven back to London. On my return home in the early hours of the morning, I must have given Mrs. P. and her wedding guests a terrible shock.

I received literally hundreds and hundreds of presents—crosses, Vishnus, horseshoes, masses of flowers and letters from all over the world when it was known what had happened. No one asked *me* for anything, not even an autograph. I think it was the first time I realized that audiences loved me for my work, and that wiped out some of the pain and the shock.

I love being alone, but even now if I am by myself on a mountain or walking in the country and I see a man in the distance I sometimes feel a moment of fear, but never on the beach near my cottage by the sea where there is nothing but peace.

Much later when I was able to put all this into perspective I realized that perhaps the two young men themselves were caught up in a Karmic debt to be paid off. I can truthfully say that I never felt hate—just surprise that we sometimes call ourselves "human" beings.

Not long after the coshing, and I don't suppose he even remembers, I ran into Alec Guinness in Knightsbridge while shopping. He looked at me, touched my face very gently with his hand, and I saw there were tears in his eyes. When I got back to my house it was full of flowers—everywhere—nearly up to the ceiling—daffodils, narcissi, tulips, blossom, spring flowers, abundant and overflowing. An inspired and generous gift from Alec.

It took a long time for my body and mind to get over the shock after the coshing. But at last I was able to go back into the play *Duel of Angels*. This was imperative in order to get my nerve back as soon as possible. The audience were very sympathetic to me. When I walked on stage for the first time, the dressing covering the cut on the left side of my head could be seen sticking out from under my wig. They clapped! Slowly I got over my fears. But I will never forget that first night of my return to the theater. All the lights had failed back stage, so we had to make up by candlelight. It was not the moment to look at my face in the mirror. Accentuated by the light from the candles, it looked strange and haunted, with its bruises, shadows and hollow eyes. Full of self-pity I burst into tears. It is interesting, however, that when it comes to the moment of appearing on stage the "real" life—grotesque or dramatic as it happens to be—is immediately cut out and the actor takes a big breath and gets on with the fantasy.

That absolute necessity to create in any of the arts is a very difficult thing to explain. It is a frightening force from within that has to be given birth. One's skin becomes thin and vulnerable like a balloon and it is necessary to cling fiercely to what one believes and to trust only oneself, in case a pin pricks the balloon and it explodes into thin air and is lost forever. It's a disease. It sometimes entails loneliness, or unpopularity, accusations of selfishness and withdrawal—and eventually the ultimate criticism: "Why don't you give up?" "Surely you could retire now and enjoy life?" But creation is joy. I think it was Shelley who said, "Dear God, let me live till I die." Creation surely is giving? The other remark that is often made to me is, "Don't you get terribly tired?" The answer is, "No, only when I am not working"; then black despair and sometimes a feeling of failure descend on me. I feel I want to curl up in bed all day with the blankets pulled over my head praying for inspiration, but when it does come, sometimes like an order from heaven, one must grasp it and use it at once—then "hand over." This does really work, coupled of course with discipline, and a certain faith in the pattern of destiny.

I have known Margot Fonteyn for many years and I would like to quote from the last paragraph in her autobiography. "If I have learnt anything it is that life forms no logical pattern—it is haphazard and full of beauties which I try to catch as they fly by. . . ." Dear Margot, of all the people I know I would say you were sent into the world by the Creator on a very much "thought-out pattern," which you are carrying out superbly, lifting us when you dance into the beauty you love so much yourself.

To bring it down now from the sublime to the ridiculous, I quote again my version of that silly verse on destiny:

I'm a creature that moves in predestined grooves
Not a car or a bus, but a *tram*.

But your tram flies, Margot.

I had played Camille on television some years before Margot danced the same part in the ballet with Nureyev. We had a discussion one day about Camille's death and how to present it. Of course it is easier for an actress as she has the words—and what immortal words they are too. As Camille falls back dying in the arms of her lover, Armand, she says with joy, just before she dies, "I am going to live, Armand, I am going to live." I played it with my arms stretching up above his head into space, not really seeing him, and I was smiling. Margot, for the ballet, did the same arm movement with joy, and the words were in her movement.

In the various artistic professions, age creeps up on us all in different ways. The dancer suffers first, as the legs are the first to go. Next comes the singer, the voice in opera. Lastly the actor, when the memory and mind collapse. Only the artist who paints can· go on and on, sitting down, dependent on no one, alone, able to float away in his dreams, still working, when the rest of us have got to the stage of just talking about it. Of course the writer is also in this category, if he can hold the pen!

There is something about artists that is always rather childish. We are ridiculously vulnerable. I sometimes think that only the people who understand this and are interested enough, or love enough, can cope with us at all. I know no one apart from myself who can giggle quite like Margot, which comes as a bit of a surprise when one has always thought of her as that exquisite creature being blown across the stage, one's eyes still following her after she has gone. Once when she and I were at a reception the gentleman in pink who announces the arrivals shouted in a loud voice as Margot approached him: "Miss Maggie Mountain," and followed it up with "Miss Ann Cod." After that, when we telephoned each other it was, "Hully, Mountain, Cod speaking." Once when she was incarcerated in some prison in South America for a night I sent her, through the ambassador, a slightly different telegram from the usual one we send on first nights in the theater, saying, "Best wishes, darling, for a short run." Incidentally, Margot gave me one of the ballet shoes that she wore for *Firebird*. It hangs on its pink satin ribbons in my flat.

It has been said that you know the truth about a man by his laugh. I hope some people know me by my giggle.

And talking of giggling, I will *never* forget an unforgettable walk down Bond Street in London with Danny Kaye, after we had had lunch.

It was a sunny day and everyone seemed to be happy.

Several people recognized Danny, of course, and stared. But even apart from recognizing him, I don't think they could have ignored us, as I was convulsed with laughter at his outrageous Walter Mitty stories, which he swore were true.

At one moment two elderly ladies passed us. They stopped, gazed at Danny, then turned around and in loud whispers said, "I tell you it's *him*." The other one answered sharply, "And I tell you it's *not*." Danny walked back and faced them. "Oh, *hello*, Auntie," he boomed. "How *extraordinary* to run into *you*. How is Cousin Frank? Did he survive his operation? That was really nasty, wasn't it? Is he OK now?" Before either lady could recover, he pressed on. "When are you coming to the States? How are the grandchildren?" The eldest lady, with a mauve rinse, stood rooted to the spot with her mouth open—startled out of her wits.

Suddenly she found her voice as Danny paused for breath. A few people in Bond Street clustered around us. "Mr. Kaye, we don't *know* you. I am *not* your aunt, you are mistaken."

Danny held up his hands to heaven, in surprise. "You are *not* Auntie?" He said. "Oh! What a *shame*. You *should* be. Give my best wishes to Frank."

He then bowed low to them both and we continued our walk. I didn't dare look back in case they had fainted right away.

I wish we could see more of Danny in England. He is such a wonderful actor, and I will never forget his performance at the Albert Hall in London as the conductor of an orchestra. It was one of the most hilarious moments I have ever experienced. And his quality of sudden sadness through the comedy is all his own and on a par with Chaplin.

*　　　*　　　*

I think it was in 1962 that I began to get an overwhelming desire to travel, and the urge has stayed with me ever since. So, when I was asked to go to Spain to make a film, I gladly accepted. It was a remake of *Captain Blood,* which Errol Flynn had starred in with Olivia De Havilland. It was now to be an epic called *The Son of Captain Blood,* and Errol Flynn's son, Sean Flynn, was to play the lead and I his mother. An American and Spanish coproduction, it was filmed in Alicante in the south of Spain. Everyone was speaking in different languages. It was like the Tower of Babel. The director was Spanish and spoke no French or English.

Sean was no actor, but I was terribly impressed with how he swung from ropes on the ship and leaped onto horses' backs at full gallop and had masses of gorgeous little girls surrounding him all the time. I think his father would have been proud of him!

The Spaniards, when they are stirred into action, do nothing by halves. The story was of the devastation of Port Royal in Jamaica by an earthquake, and everybody got over-excited about the trick photography that was needed for the earthquake, flooding, and fires that had to be shown on the screen. I, as the widow of Captain Blood, ran our big plantation with my son. We filmed a real fire; I was in the middle of the plantation with all my "slaves," but they threw so much gasoline over the sugarcane that it caught alight in a very big way and we were trapped where the cameras couldn't even see us. If the wind hadn't changed, the film would have finished there and then as we would have been cinders! Another time the American producer took a small unused church, removed the roof and put eight cameras on top. They then took out the windows and replaced them with vast water pumps and filled the church with about two hundred and fifty black people and me. We were filming the earthquake and the flood that followed, and we were supposed to be caught inside the church, unable to get out till my son (Sean) arrived, forced the door open and saved us all. The scene had to be taken in one "shot" as repetition was impossible, hence all the cameras on the roof. On "action" I was up at the altar praying, with two adorable little black children, one under each arm. The water was pouring in from the pumps and the congregation of black "slaves" was standing waist deep in it when the little boy under my arm shouted above the noise, "*Je voudrais faire un pipi*," then solmenly did it into the flood while we all waited in silence. It certainly was his moment. We then continued filming.

To keep me warm and dry in the water, I had been given long mackintosh trousers to wear under my crinoline. Suddenly the Spanish director went mad and ordered the pumps to be speeded up and made stronger. There was absolute chaos as water gushed in, flooding everything, and we couldn't get out. Everyone was screaming. We rushed for the door; people were up to their necks in water and terrified. It was real panic. Someone clutched me, and I went down on my face between the pews and couldn't get up because of the weight of my soaking long skirt. The children were grabbed from me. Sean couldn't save us, story or no story, as the door had jammed. It really was a nightmare, but at the back of my mind through it all I kept thinking, "*What* a scene they will have—it's all for real. What a scoop."

After years, it seemed, they got the pumps turned off and the door open, and dear Sean was so worried he just picked me up in his arms and carried me like a baby out of the church.

Next day we all hurried in excited anticipation to see the rushes on the screen but, as so often happens in our job, the truth was not so strange as the fiction. It meant absolutely nothing, and we had to repeat the whole thing calmly in the studio in Madrid using close-ups while the background was tricked. This time it had true excitement and was really moving! When they came to my close-up, showing the agony we had to go through, the cameraman refused to photograph me (shades of Hollywood) and kept saying, "*Vena, vena.*" Exhausted, I looked up cheerfully and said, "Oh, yes, *vino, vino,* what a good idea." He was actually referring to the vein under my eye, which I had had since the mugging, not a delicious glass of wine.

After all this hilarious drama was over I couldn't help wondering what was I up to and where was I going and why, but the episode brought me one great bonus. I met a friend for life in the late Johnny Kitzmiller, the well-known Negro actor, who taught me so much wisdom about living. In him I had the rare experience of meeting a complete human being, and it is worth going through almost anything for that.

I was soon on the move again. This time I was asked to be in a film being shot in Prague. It was quite an experience. I should have known what was in store, because as I landed at the airport I saw in the distance the late Donald Wolfit whom I did not know, catching his plane back to England, having finished his part in the film. He raised his hat and shouted to me, "Best of British luck to you, Miss Todd. You certainly will need it."

It was a coproduction between Czechoslovakia and England. I was playing a Czech, my first real character role. In the film I was the drunken wife of one of their top

Czech actors. My high cheekbones can turn me into a Slav, as I was to find later in Moscow.

Rudolf Hrusinsky was the name of the actor who was the star; he was known as the Laurence Olivier of Czechoslovakia. He was portly and bald and acted like a Marlon Brando with his mouth nearly closed and his head down. Of course, he was speaking in Czech and I was answering in English, so I had to concentrate with everything I had on his mouth. When he stopped speaking, I pounced and delivered my part and prayed I was making sense. (This was all to be dubbed into our different languages later on.) He had no sense of humor whatsoever, which was a pity as it might have saved the situation and jollied things up a bit. We worked in a Russian studio with no limit on time, so we were filming into all hours.

My first scene with Mr. Hrusinsky was as his wife, drunk, and in a very small bed (it would never have been allowed in England at that time). We settled down and lay stiffly side by side. The director then made a long speech in Czech, translated by someone in a breathless whisper for me. It was all about how famous I was— Shakespeare and all that. Then Mr. H. took over and, without moving anything but his head, he turned on the pillow and delivered another speech about how charming I was, which didn't make sense as I had only just met him, and my face as his drunken wife was far from charming. He finished by saying what an honor it was to act with me, and that he wished he could speak my language (so did I). I then turned *my* head toward him on the pillow and delivered exactly the same speech back to him, in English, translated again in a whisper. We then sat up and bowed to each other.

The director called out something like "start," and from then on it was just a bad dream, or perhaps a big joke.

The film, *90 Degrees in the Shade,* was shown at the Berlin Film Festival but was never released in England (except that recently I think it was shown on late-night television here). It was all rather a shame, as nowadays they have such brilliant directors and producers working in Czechoslovakia in such difficult circumstances, and I would love to go back to their beautiful city of Prague and work there again. Well, maybe one day.

CHAPTER 10

Thunder in Heaven

"If you can see it, begin it; action has
genius, power, magic in it."
—GOETHE

After my return from Prague, I experienced a turning point in my life, though I didn't know this at the time. One night I had what most people would call a dream, but it was in fact for me a vision. I am absolutely certain we "travel" sometimes in our sleep and that dreams are used by higher powers, either to help those in the same state or to gather knowledge and guidance from the subconscious to bring back to earth. Some advanced people can remember where they have been and what they have been told.

I think Rupert Brooke was talking about this when he spoke of "Sleep and high places" in his beautiful poem "The Great Lover," when describing "These I have loved."

On this particular night, I woke up suddenly as if I had been tapped on the shoulder. I lay quite still in the dark, waiting. Then I felt little vibrations running up and down my spine and I started to float! Very slowly a white light like a large white ball appeared on the ceiling—I thought for a moment it was a car passing, or something in the street outside. Then as I lay there, not a bit frightened, the light changed shape and got longer and longer like a banner being unfurled above my head. As I watched, the light formed itself very slowly into large letters, and a word appeared written across the ceiling. The word was *Khatmandu* (spelled with the *h* as used to be common). It stayed there for about seven seconds and then slowly faded out.

I turned on the light by my bed and tried to work out what had happened. It had seemed like a summons. My geography has never been good, so in the morning I had to telephone my son, who always has the answer, and ask where Katmandu was. This was fourteen years ago, and Nepal was much more isolated then from the rest of the world. People didn't know as much about it was we do now. It began to worry me. What was it all about? And what was I meant to do? I then set out to buy all sorts of books about the country, anything I could lay my hands on, and after that I visited the Nepalese Embassy.

I had no acting commitments just then, and I began to tell people of my plan, which was to go to Nepal—by myself. They thought I was mad. I had never been anywhere abroad on my own, not even to Paris, and I had certainly never been East. Anyone who knew anything about Nepal agreed with the travel books that it was very rough going when you got there.

I didn't know why I was going but the "sign" had been so extraordinary that I felt once more that it must be my destiny, so I bought long woollen underwear, bed socks, vests, boots, medicines, sleeping bag, etcetera, and flew

off to Katmandu. I didn't know then it was the start of a
new job for me. I was changing gears again.

It was all very strange when I arrived in Nepal, but oh!
how beautiful when we started to come down in our tiny
plane onto the vivid green patch that was the airport. The
emerald jewel of Katmandu below was surrounded by the
highest mountains on earth. It was evening and the
Himalayas were ice green, especially Everest and Kan-
gchenjunga. Annapurna, being female, was pink and
sensual. The Nepalese believe in the gods and goddesses
that are the mountains. You could be knifed if you
proclaimed that you had climbed Dhaulagiri—where the
goddess reigns. No one must "mount" a goddess. A friend
of mine climbed to the top of this mountain, 26,800 feet,
but he never mentioned it in Nepal. He always said he
hadn't managed the last hundred feet.

The flight was a bit scary for me, especially as I was
traveling alone and don't care for flying anyway. We were
in a plane that held eight people, and from Delhi we had
to fly below the Himalayas, like a bus turning corners,
with the mountains towering over us on either side. We
were strapped together in two's. I was with a Sikh who
gave me courage, till I heard an Englishman's voice at
the back say: "What are the Nepalese pilots like?" Back
came the answer, "Improving."

On arrival I stayed with the British consul in Katmandu for a week, then went to a so-called hotel. I went
into the kitchen there and found cockroaches running all
over the table, as Hindus won't take life. I asked if it was
possible to give us the goat meat without the rather
disgusting unappetizing gravy, as people from the West
found it difficult to eat. The cook answered: "Do you
know how difficult it is for us to give you *meat* at all, we

never touch it, ourselves, only rice." I felt like a cannibal.

I was asked later to attend the dawn sacrifice of the buffaloes and could hardly live through it. In a closed court open to the sky three hundred animals were killed for sacrifice. The army was lined up with raised rifles, which they shot into the air as each buffalo was beheaded in honor of the sacrifice of the dead. I noticed a pure white egret flying in circles in the blue sky overhead—the soul of the animals?

It was a horrifying sight, but the Nepalese kill only for sacrifice to their gods; even the poorest will bring a precious chicken, so who are we in the West to criticize? We kill to eat and we do it—ashamed to look—behind closed doors in an abbattoir.

A little later I was able to leave the hotel, as I was lucky enough to have an invitation to stay in the palace of one of the ranas and his ranee. On my first day I was received at the palace. I arrived by trishaw, and a servant escorted me, not into the palace, to my surprise, but up a little hill. When I arrived at the top he bowed and disappeared. At my feet were a prayer mat, their Bible, the Bhagavad-Gita, and our Bible. I took my shoes off and sat down in the lotus position and in the silence gazed at the giants of peace that surrounded us, and prayed and prayed that I would be given guidance on what I was meant to do there. Then I opened our Bible. It was Easter Day in the West, and I read about Christ and the Resurrection and remembered my illness and the day I had died. I wondered for what reason I had to come back.

I don't know how long it was, but I heard a little bell and the servant returned. He guided me down the hill and I entered the palace. As we went up each floor a different instrument was played, like a flute, then on the next floor a drum, etcetera, to warn the private apartments that we were approaching.

The rana was an uncle of the king. He came toward me, an extremely good-looking man, gray-haired, tall and dressed in pink-and-red robes. I did the *namaste*, low for deep respect. The rana's first words were, "You found peace? I know it is an important day for you." How many of us know *their* important days, I wonder?

The ranas in the old days were feudal families and warlords with great power in Nepal. Their palace had three hundred servants who worked on a rota. There were no windows, but large shutters which, when opened, looked out to the most wonderful view in the world—the Himalayas. The bath, from England, was at the top of the main staircase in a little enclosure facing the mountains. It had no running water; water was carried in buckets. It was a place for meditation as well as washing.

The rana and ranee sometimes received their guests in their palatial bedroom. It had two very large fourposters at either end and prayer mats beside them, and when they "went into grace" a little bell was rung and we had to retire and leave them alone.

They were truly marvelous to me and I learned many things of the wisdom of the East from them, and we used to have long discussions about everything. The rana was educated at public school and university. But in Nepal his astrologer came to him every morning before he saw his secretary to tell him what was right as shown by the stars for his program that day. His favorite play was Shakespeare's *Julius Caesar,* and he seemed to know the whole play by heart.

The women in his family were not allowed, however

traveled and sophisticated they were, to appear or eat with anyone when they had their periods.

I was very thrilled when an arrangement was made for me to fly with an interpreter to Pokhara, a mountain village at the foot of the Himalayas. We set off in a tiny plane, again with no radar. A rattle was swung around and around on the patch where we were to land (which was the airport) to announce our arrival and chase off the buffaloes and camels, who were standing in our way. On touching down all that was to be seen or heard in this high and isolated place was a blind man playing a flute. He stood under a tree, hoping to make a quick fortune on predicting if we should ever get off again, I presume.

I was told a rather nice story. Two Nepalese were watching a transport plane landing on its way to Benares in India. The back of the plane was opened up and two small jeeps were pulled out. One Nepalese was heard saying to the other, "What are *those?*" The other, not knowing but showing off, answered, "Oh, they are baby airplanes before their wings have grown."

At the time I went to Pokhara one hardly ever saw any Europeans or Americans—even embassy staff in Katmandu seldom visited there: so I was surprised to be hailed by a fat black lady as I got off the plane: "Hey, I am Margaret Sullivan, Ohio, USA, who are you?"

I answered, "I am Ann Todd, London, England."

"Not a relation of *the* Ann Todd?" she said.

She made my day and we embraced. This canceled out a conversation I had had in Delhi on our way out while signing autographs, which always embarrasses me. A small lady this time—very British in hat and gloves— stood by me all the time without speaking, till at last I turned to her and said, "Can I do anything for you? Would you like my autograph?"

She answered, "No. I am very disappointed in you. I saw *The Seventh Veil* nine times and you were so beautiful and sad and mysterious and out here you have done nothing but laugh."

You can't please everyone!

Because of the occasional impossibility of washing my hair, I always travel with a wig for emergency. In Pokhara there was almost no privacy, and when I took off on one occasion, the little crowd around my door screamed and ran away—they thought I had taken my head off.

One night in this same village we had a thrilling and Wagnerian experience—living through the most incredible thunderstorm. Nepal is sometimes called the "Roof of the World" and it certainly felt like it. I was sleeping in a long corrugated hut provided for travelers with ten gentlemen. The storm raged around us. I was extremely frightened and crawled to the bottom of my sleeping bag with, I am ashamed to say it, Edward, my teddy bear, while all hell hit the tin roof. It sounded as if we were under rifle fire. The birds, also in panic, came through any holes they could find for shelter and flew wildly around above our heads. Everything ceased with the dawn and we all emerged. We did look a funny bunch— Indians, Sikhs, my Nepalese interpreter and me, dressed in an extraordinary assortment of clothes, pyjamas, robes, turbans, woolly caps, etcetera. I looked the funniest and hardly human. We faced the mountains, put our hands together, bowed and did the *namaste*, to say thank you, I presumed, for our deliverance and good morning to each individual mountain and then went back to our hut to sleep. Later a gong was rung and everyone rushed to another hut for breakfast, with cockroaches leaping about. All except me. I was an "untouchable" and had to wait till they had finished.

In Pokhara I met a very attractive young Nepalese couple on their honeymoon. The bride was dying, and her great desire was to leave this world while in the mountains close to her gods, so her loved one had married her and brought her there. They seemed so happy all the time—she was radiant. She died while we were there. The husband, though desperately sad, had such strong belief and was so certain she would be happy when she "woke up," as they call it, that I felt she was still with us. They believe that they go on to a continuation of this life but something much better.

I came across this again in Katmandu, where there was a small hospital run by a very special American lady. When she arrived in Nepal she told me she was ready to change everyone and win them over to her belief, but very soon she realized this was wrong, so when a Nepalese was sick or seemed to be dying she would ask them if they wanted to die or live. If the answer was die, she would help them "over." If they asked to live (usually the more progressive ones) she tried to cure them.

I met her when I was asked to sit with a young mother who had had a Caesarean operation. She was perfectly healthy and the baby was fine, but she turned her face to the wall because she had been "touched" and thought her destiny had been interfered with, so she wanted to die. Although I stayed with her and kept repeating the few words in Nepali that I had learned ("Ramro"— beautiful) and held her baby out to her and cuddled it, she "went" in that extraordinary way the Easterners have of carrying out that which they think is right.

Nepal has so much to teach us, in ways that perhaps

we don't understand. I found simplicity, innocence and happiness there that we are losing in the West. Of course progress is inevitable, but what is the price we are having to pay for it? One sometimes wonders.

Meanwhile I realized that all my ideas were beginning to unfold themselves in my head, but how to present them, that was the problem. I had kept a diary, day by day, while I was in Nepal, and my love for this place was so great that I knew I must show to the world what I myself had seen and experienced. But again I wondered how. I was not a writer; I had never made a film; all I knew about was acting. It may sound dramatic, but the answer was made clear one evening while I was sitting cross-legged on the little hill outside the rana's palace. I was facing those great silent mountains, clothed in mystery. The color of the sky was beyond description as the sun went down over Machapuchara, Annapurna and, still further away, Everest. Then I remember the exciting moment when a broad streak of emerald green suddenly appeared. It pierced through the whole vast panorama like a meteor demanding attention. It was as if Lohengrin himself were touching the universe with his holy sword. The strength and magnitude were overpowering but I got my answer, which was that I should make a film, a kind of documentary to show what Nepal has to offer to all of us.

After I had been in Nepal two weeks I received the summons to the palace for my audience with His Divine Majesty, King Majhendra. The various ministers in Katmandu and all the people who had helped to pull this meeting off were so excited that I began to be very nervous. Suppose I had to return to England without permission to film?

It was up to me now. For the first time I realized how alone I was. But the vision I had had in England which had brought me here had also somehow indicated that all would be well.

One night I was invited to a dinner party at the Chinese Embassy. There were many important people present and everyone seemed astonished that I had got an audience so soon. Most people, they told me, have to wait months.

The rana teased me and said the king probably wanted to have a look at me, as up till then His Majesty had not met an actress or even had a private audience with a woman. One must remember this was more than fifteen years ago.

At the end of the dinner the beautiful and fragile-looking wife of the Chinese ambassador stood up and, with a lovely smile toward all the ladies present, said: "Shall we leave the gentlemen to their pot, and retire to wash our noses." I hope so much no one ever told her and she is still making the same speech!

The next day in preparation for my audience with the king I washed my hair in the bath with no plug, my heel on the hole to stop the water running away—and with the usual four cans of tepid water brought up by the Nepalese servant. The bath had a tap and looked grand, but nothing worked. Then I hung my head out of the window for it to dry. Below me in the street stood a lovely girl stripped to the waist washing her hair under the communal tap. She tossed her head back and shook it from side to side; she caught my eye and we waved to each other. She then started to clean her teeth. No one took any notice of her and there were certainly no wolf whistles. These people, whom some call primitive, have a great dignity and respect for women.

The mountain people of Nepal look tougher and healthier than in India, and so they should, living so high up in that scintillating air. Only twenty-five years ago they were completely isolated from everyone; no one visited them except mountaineers and a few other adventurous people. Even when I was there, there were few Westerners and I felt as if I were entering a strange hidden world completely encircled by the giant Himalayas.

The Nepalese smile most of the time, and though it is obvious that they live in great poverty there is an overall happiness that seems to shine out of their faces. I called on several houses of the very poor. The top room is for the family, who sleep on straw mats. The meditation room is beside it, sometimes only the size of a closet. Down below on the ground floor are the animals. All washing is done in the street; it's quite usual to see the small children in the early morning doing their business in the gutter, sitting in rows. I don't know what the grownups do, but I do know the contrasts in Katmandu are extreme. You can turn a corner in the street and see an exquisite Greek statue, and the next moment you may have the contents of a bucket poured over your head.

Someone told me when I first arrived that if I should hear one of the big bells being rung it meant somebody was asking the gods for an answer to his prayers. When it rang, the people in the fields could hear it and would stop work and pray. It was suggested that I should ring it for my film. Feeling very self-conscious I did so, especially as now I was about to meet His Divine Majesty. Maybe my prayer had been heard.

The Nepalese are a very religious people. I believe it's the only place in the world where the two great religions Buddhism and Hinduism sometimes worship in the same temples. What a pity the West doesn't copy their example.

Most people, though, worship at the holy river in Katmandu at Pashupatinath, holding their arms up to the sky and the sun. They believe that God is everywhere, especially out of doors in nature. At Bodnath, in the center of Katmandu, there is a large figure of the Lord Buddha; flags stretch from this figure down to earth, and the people believe that when the flags wave in the breeze it is their prayers rising up to him.

The Nepalese have a charming idea about mad people. In the West, if the old become senile or "difficult," we shove them into homes and hide them away. In Nepal they are cherished and loved. The Nepalese believe that when they are in this condition they are floating between heaven and earth and they therefore become agents and a link between themselves and God; and so, of course, they are very important.

The great day arrived for my audience with King Majhendra. I had been told that I was expected to "dress up" and wear a long garment with my arms covered. So at 3 P.M. in blinding heat I put on my long cream silk evening dress, which Norman Hartnell had designed for me years ago, and my great-grandmother's cream lace coat with sleeves and high neck, and any bit of jewelry I had with me.

When I was in Nepal there were very few cars, just a few jeeps or trishaws. These are the same as a rickshaw except that instead of a man running in front there is a man on a bicycle.

However, a car was sent for me from the palace. It was a white Rolls and the chauffeur was dressed in white. I had been told I was to come alone. As we approached the palace gates I felt as if I were playing in *Cinderella;* it was like a fairy tale. Over the entrance gates there seemed to be masses of cotton wool, looking like snow. This they called the Mountains of the Moon.

I was shown into a small anteroom where I sat down and waited, feeling extremely hot. After half an hour an army officer, obviously very important with medals thick on his chest, came in and signed to me to follow him.

I had been instructed to keep my eyes on the ground until His Majesty spoke to me. He is divine in his own country, as the Nepalese believe he is a direct descendant from the god Vishnu.

I entered what seemed, through my downcast eyes, an enormous room. On the left I thought I saw a large stuffed bear, and on my right, far away, a pair of feet. The gentleman with the medals shouted, I thought unnecessarily loudly, "Miss Ann Todd of England, Your Majesty."

I stepped forward and put my hands together, palms touching—the *namaste*—then raised them to my forehead and lowered myself as low as I could. I followed this with a sweeping curtsey for England. The king spoke and I raised my eyes. Somehow I felt a little let down, as he was dressed in ordinary Nepalese clothes. I had imagined him in his beautiful robes and plumed headdress of feathers.

We then sat on a very small sofa. I tried to squash myself into the corner. He asked me why I wanted to make a film of Nepal. He had a lovely voice and spoke very quietly, with hardly a trace of an accent. I replied that I wanted to show the world the simplicity and innocence of his beautiful country and their peace.

My audience lasted half an hour. Then, oh joy, he gave me permission to film. There was then a long pause. I looked at my feet. I don't know where His Majesty looked.

In my experience with royalty, they dismiss you when the time is up, but as nothing happened I said, "Would Your Divine Majesty like me to go?"

"Yes," he answered immediately.

I got up and started to back out, wondering whether I was going to fall over my long skirt. Then the king held out his hand to me. I practically ran to him and we stood facing each other. The people of Nepal are small in stature so our eyes were on the same level. I said: "Your Majesty, *Dhanyabad—ma kushi chu.*" Which means, "Thank you. I am very happy."

The king answered, "Oh, so you speak our language."

I said, "Oh, no, only three sentences, Your Majesty."

He smiled and said, "But you have only said one sentence. What are the other two?"

I answered, "In the words of my profession, Your Majesty, I am afraid I have dried up."

His Divine Majesty then laughed, and I went back in the white Rolls to the rana's palace, where everyone was overjoyed about the film and I was given a sherry—the first and last drink I had in Nepal as women don't imbibe.

On my last day I went to say goodbye to the rana and his family, who had helped me so much. I had to try to hide my emotions. I wanted to stay forever in this beautiful place.

We gathered in one of the big rooms in the palace; the light was beginning to go and everything looked misty green and ghostly. The servants floated in and out in their silent peaceful way and my eyes kept returning to the mountains outside—those mountains—so old—so icy cold—so full of wisdom as they looked down on us.

The door opened and the ranee came in, looking beautiful in her gold-and-red sari, her black hair piled up on her head with jewels. She was carrying a parcel—a present for me on a velvet cushion. Behind her came her ladies, looking like silent moths in the half-light. I felt I was in a play—it all seemed so unreal.

The ranee's English wasn't very good, but the rana told me as I unpacked the parcel that it was her own cape, one of her honeymoon presents all those years ago. It was made of their strange green padded cotton (which is impossible to find anywhere else) embroidered all around with the serpents of Nepal in thick gold. She put it around my shoulders and I didn't dare speak—one doesn't have to throw one's arms around people to show affection. In her silence and her look at me, she gave me love—never to be forgotten.

One day I would go back—I knew.

When I returned to London having spent three and a half weeks in heaven—Nepal—I had no idea what to do next so, armed with the precious letter of permission to make a film from the King, I finally went to see my bank manager. I asked him, rather cheekily, for a loan to start me off on my project.

He replied, "We know you as an actress, Miss Todd, but what experience have you had? What do you know about producing a film?"

I said, "Nothing." I could see my "heaven" fading away and continued desperately, "But I *promise* I will find a producer to help me and will do all the nonmoney side myself."

He said, with a rather severe note in his voice, "How much?"

I took a big breath (because of my overdraft) and answered "$33,000 to film in Nepal." I shut my eyes.

"Good God," he murmured. "Where?"

I got it. There and then I christened my precious child *Thunder in Heaven.*

I will always be grateful to Lloyds Bank for having faith

in me. When I got outside I was so shaken at what I had achieved and the responsibility it entailed, that I decided not to buy the hat I had seen in Fenwicks around the corner and returned home by bus instead of taking a taxi.

Two and a half months later I was back in Nepal with a small film unit to make the first of my Diary Documentary films. I now had for the first time great responsibility as regards my work. I had made as many arrangements as possible on my first visit, such as fixing up jeeps for carrying our equipment—tents, maps, boots for climbing, permission for filming the sacred temples, etcetera. I had also chosen what I thought the most important things in the country to fit in with the story I was to tell. I was determined to break with the usual standard documentary and travelogue films that were being shown at that time and had written a thirty-page synopsis of my ideas, which had been sent to King Majhendra and the various ministers concerned. I had also been able to concoct a rough shooting script.

At last we started to film. It was a most thrilling moment for me and I found it almost impossible to take in what I was doing and where. My daughter often used to say, when she was a child, "Mummy, I did it all by myself." I had no one to say this to in Nepal but at this moment I said it in a whisper, secretly, and felt rather proud.

There were many difficulties, of course, as I not only appeared in the film myself but also had to spend a lot of time struggling with the crowds. They were all so cheerful and happy and smiled all the time. I think they thought it was a lovely game and considered us all very funny. A few of them ran away from the camera when it was pointed at them, being quite certain it was the evil eye, but most of them rushed at it, pressing their faces so close that it was impossible to go ahead. I had to try to control these happy-go-lucky people who all wanted to be "in the game." I put my hands together in the *namaste* and pleaded with them with my eyes and smile, saying in English, "Please, will you go away from the camera," but they wouldn't. I had to rush quickly back to the camera director to be filmed myself before returning to face the advancing, laughing Nepalese again, and to take up my position as a sort of policewoman to keep order. Our unit was too small to spare any of its important members to deal with this situation.

Everybody in Katmandu was most helpful to us, including the British Embassy and the Nepalese ministers. I don't go all the way with women's liberation. I think we can usually get what we want in the old-fashioned way. Anyway, it seems to work all right with my Diary Documentary films, or perhaps it is that the ministers, or those in control who help me, are anxious for my sanity and think I need protection, so just give way! I don't complain. Especially if the result is what I want and it makes the gentlemen happy.

The worst gamble of all was the worry of sending back to England the filming we had done in order to check if it was all right for color, light, etcetera. We had no idea till we actually got home six weeks later if we *had* a film at all.

The first day it was shown to me in London—I think it was five hours of separate pieces of film—I sat alone in the cinema and prayed and prayed. I needn't have bothered; it soon became clear that a loud "thank you" was all that was needed. It was breathtakingly beautiful—the Himalayas covered in snow towering over us. I just sat there, living it all again and thinking of a Greek phrase a gentleman friend I knew had once given me: *o epimenon nika* (the persistent one conquers) and I felt without conceit that perhaps I could use it now.

My confidence was soon to be dashed to the ground. The few distributors I showed the film to said it didn't fit into any "slot" as it wasn't a documentary or a travelogue, and some said it was too moving as a "short" to come before a feature film. I tramped round Soho and Wardour Street, showing my "jewel" to various hard-faced cigar-smoking distributors who agreed it was beautiful, artistic, but they weren't interested.

I had only one person who helped me, Dick Marden, a well-known editor. He sat for hours in the editing rooms while I sat on the floor drinking gallons of coffee, and he coaxed out of me the narration, bit by bit, and then cut it into the film. He kept me calm and gave me courage—and hope. Then I had to decide on the music. I didn't know where to go and no one helped, but of course miracles do happen and I certainly had one. I was in a small gramophone shop one day, feeling terribly depressed, and it was pouring rain. I remember so well the old man who served me. He was small with rather long gray hair and a droopy moustache. He seemed so kind and gentle with me.

Some people have real feelings in their eyes, and some have the opposite, what David Lean used to call "button eyes" just stamped on their faces—"They do nothing for a close-up or for my film," he would say. The old gentleman in the gramophone and music shop certainly had not got button eyes. I told him how worried was and asked if he had any Nepalese music. He hadn't, only Indian, which is not the same. Then he said: "Why don't you ask Malcolm Williamson?"

To my shame, not being of the music world, I hadn't heard of him at that time. When I got home I rushed to the telephone book and looked up the now-famous Malcolm Williamson's number and rang him.

He answered the phone. I told him all my troubles. He answered, "I will be around in twenty minutes."

I have learned through my life that the people, big or small, who say, "Well, yes but . . ." or "At the moment, too busy," or "It's a bad moment," are those who never succeed or, more important, are never great. I think it was Churchill who said: "There is always Time for what one *feels* is important."

I had taken an 8-mm. film when I was in Nepal. The camera was extremely expensive and had lots of gadgets, and up till then I had only taken half a dozen photographs in my life with a cheap Kodak, so when I filmed with this complicated camera with close-ups, middle shots, distance, etcetera, I closed my eyes and clicked. But it finished up not a bad effort, which staggered my family and surprised me as well. This I showed to Malcolm Williamson. Then on the spot he said, "I will compose the music for you." Malcolm asked nothing of me—it was a gift—and what a wonderful gift. He took one theme and wove it around in different ways all through the film. It was authentic Nepalese music, but it was also commercial, which is extremely important when you think of the wide audiences films play to—trapped audiences, not like television watchers, who, if they are bored, can go and make a cup of tea. Then perhaps the miracle I claimed was granted.

The film was finally shown to Her Majesty the Queen and Prince Philip and their guests during Ascot week and then went out on distribution. And so my "series" was launched, first by Home Entertainments, Lord Brabourne's Company, and eventually by the Rank Organisation; so, funnily enough, I had come round full circle and was back again with Rank who had made me a star.

I have now made many Diary Documentaries and have traveled to Egypt, Persia, Greece, Australia, Jordan and, two years ago, Iona, the Hebridean island. John Turner took over as my producer after the first three films, and we have been together for many years. I couldn't have done anything without him. I get backing now from the countries where the documentaries are made as, apart from the film, they get a lot of publicity worldwide. My first job on visiting each country, always initially alone and as their guest, is to woo them for the money for the film, having written a short synopsis on what I see and feel. Each film runs half an hour and comes on before the feature film on the cimema screen. The documentaries are abstract, timeless and nonpolitical. I am in them all and each country is seen through my eyes. I write the narration and speak it. Most exciting of all, I attend the editing sessions with the professional editor at the end. Later they will be shown on television. To my astonishment three of the films are now showing again for the third time on general release, so all the thought and care I put into making them timeless and detailed has paid off. I was thrilled too that some of them have appeared at festivals, in Berlin, Cork and San Sebastian.

It was pointed out to me only a few years ago that this series has managed to catch hold of those precious things that we are fast losing in our own civilization: *Jordan,* silence, the desert; *Nepal,* innocence and simplicity; *Iona,* light over darkness; *Australia,* space; *Persia,* wonderment; *Greece,* hope and faith; *Egypt,* glory and dignity. Later, having seen them run on one after the other myself, I realized this was true.

I hope to make two more, and last year I visited Russia

and Israel to talk about it. It's a wonderful life, granted to so few, working in exciting countries—all expenses paid. It is a shame that I am so shy and find it quite impossible to make a speech, because more people should know about and share all this with me.

We were having a private showing of the film made in the Hebrides last year at my local cinema, and a few important people were invited. The manager was standing outside the cinema waiting to receive them, when a rather sad-looking lady with her shopping basket over her arm went up to him and said, "What's going on?" The manager explained that it was a private showing of one of my films and she said, "I have traveled everywhere with Ann Todd, can I go in?" He thought, of course, that I knew her, so waved her through. Afterward she went up to him and said, "I have now been with her to every place she has visited, without leaving home. Please thank her."

I thought this was one of the greatest compliments I have ever had.

CHAPTER 11

Of Gods and Kings

Afpter *Thunder in Heaven,* my first documentary, was born I formed my own company and began to think about my next project.

Someone suggested Greece, and I jumped at it. I had been there eight years before for a blissfully happy holiday on a glamorous yacht sailing around the islands. The party had consisted entirely of Greeks, including the Greek actress Melina Mercouri. I shared a cabin with Melina and learned a lot more than I had known before about life! She has style and drive, two qualities that I admire very much. Although at that time she spoke very little English we got on wonderfully well together. In fact, to the amusement of the rest of the party, one calm hot day Melina and I took it in turns to recite Lady Macbeth dressed in our bikinis. She had played the part at the Herodotus Atticus Theatre in Athens at almost the same

Top left, at a Hollywood premiere with Loretta Young's ermine cape; *Top right*, Whisky and me playing.

With Ray Milland in *So Evil My Love*.

PARAMOUNT

The Snows of Kilimanjaro, a televisio[n] spectacular that won an Emmy. Me an[d] Robert Ryan.

Rehearsing with Cary Grant for a radio program, *Suspense*.

With Charles Laughton in *The Paradine Case*.

The Paradine Case. This photograph once won a prize! While the scenery was being changed between scenes, Greg took me in his arms and said, "I didn't really mean what I said!" Meanwhile in the background Hitchcock sneezed. We were all "doing our own thing."

The Paradine Case with Gregory Peck.

Hitchcock directing *The Paradine Case*.

Left, with Claude Rains and Trevor Howard after a happy lunch before starting on *One Woman's Story*; *Above*, Working with David Lean on *One Woman's Story*; *Below*, *One Woman's Story* with Claude Rains.

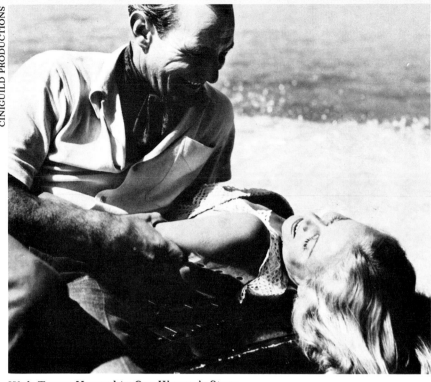

With Trevor Howard in *One Woman's Story*.

With Trevor Howard filming *One Woman's Story* in Chamonix.

One Woman's Story.

The court scene from *Madeleine*, directed by David Lean, at that time my husband. CINIGUILD PRODUCTIONS

Filming *Madeleine* on the beach at Cornwall. This is just before the horse bolted. CINIGUILD PRODUCTIONS

time that I was playing it at the Old Vic; as I believe (as most actors do) in the superstition that to recite *Macbeth* away from the theater brings bad luck, I don't know why the yacht didn't sink there and then.

In fact, we actually very nearly did sink going through a terrible storm in the Aegean. Melina and I had to be tied down in our bunks for safety. We lost our lifeboat, and Paddy Leigh Fermor's large, heavy, best-selling book *Mani*, which he had just given me, fell on my head in the cabin and nearly knocked me out. Melina moaned and sobbed, and I tried desperately to keep a stiff upper lip for Scotland! It didn't help when the Greek captain came down to us, spread his arms wide, shook his head, and then put his hands together in prayer, while his eyes rolled up to heaven. But we made it to the island of Mykonos.

Our return journey was less dramatic, by public transport in a large ship carrying hundreds of sheep and goats.

Before this drama happened, we had been to Delphi and the great Greek actress Paxinou had joined us. Our host took us up to the Amphitheatre with its extraordinary sound effects invented all those thousands of years ago and still a secret.

Paxinou went first and stood on the spot where you can whisper and be heard by three thousand people from the back of the arena. She recited *Iphigenia in Aulis* by Euripides in Greek to a theater empty except for us. As she stood there I seemed to see her in the robes of ancient Greece, as her marvelous voice reverberated around the rocks of Parnassus.

Then Melina recited, in French, *Phèdre* by Racine. And then it was my turn. They wanted Shakespeare, of course, but I couldn't move. I just sat there trembling and kept whispering, "I can't—I daren't—in front of all the gods grouped around us at this moment, I can't."

Our host, a philosopher, came and sat beside me, held my hand and patted it as if I were a child. "I understand," he said. "Perhaps you have been here before. The theater is full of ghosts. You can't avoid this." What the others thought, I don't know, and I didn't really understand what our Greek host meant and felt a fool.

But eight years later I was to come back to Delphi to make my film *Thunder of the Gods*.

While we were preparing my Greek film in 1965, I did a play in the theater, *The Vortex* by Noël Coward. Noël was a great friend of mine. He was one of the most generous people I have ever met, generous with his time, his energy and interest in people. A typical example of his kindness was when he lent David Lean and myself his beautiful home in Jamaica for our honeymoon.

I remember once telling him I had seen an understudy take over at a moment's notice in a play in Edinburgh and how marvelous she was. Noël dropped everything and dashed up to Scotland at once to see her performance.

I don't cry when people die. I think it is such a wonderful progression for them to go on and continue in the Spirit World. I was in the kitchen boiling an egg when I heard on the radio that Noël had died. This time I did sit down and cry, partly for the loss of what he represented—style, professionalism and discipline in the theater, and that we will sadly miss. An era had gone.

I had played in *The Vortex* before on television with David McCallum, as my son, in the part Coward played originally. David was brilliant and I loved playing with him.

I don't think people realize what an enormous difference it makes if two personalities in a play or film have rapport and understanding and like each other. We are all very vulnerable creatures as we stand up bravely and strip ourselves of ourselves. In fact, I think that when filming it is rather important that the director be in love with one for the duration of the film. It makes one feel good, more confident. He is really the only audience, in shadow behind the camera, as one stands in front of him like a butterfly pinned in light.

Only very few artists have the cheek and temerity to question the director, like the blonde glamor girl who required thirty-five takes of one small scene. When the exhausted and desperate director said, "OK, OK, honey, it's coming along nicely—just one more try," she answered crossly: "What do you mean, *coming* along nicely, that's *it!*" and added in an aside, "Funny, he can't make up his mind which take to choose."

The Vortex was played at the Yvonne Arnaud Theatre. It was a very big challenge for me, especially the beginning of the play, as it is mostly high comedy, which I felt I had never been able to do. In fact, when I was learning the part, Dorothy Tutin, who is a marvelous comedienne, tried to help me on timing to get the laughs. Also, I prefer to play roles that make their first entrance quietly and grow as the play goes on. Florence in *The Vortex* had to sweep on with enormous glamor and wit, having been talked about for a long time before she appears as being so beautiful and entrancing. I remember standing in the wings one night and telling the maid in the play, who was about to announce me, and who was also my understudy, that I was praying to faint so she could take over.

She whispered back: "But the theater is full, boxes and all, wanting to see you." Which made it that much worse.

I seriously believe I must have suffered some time far back in history in the Coliseum in Rome, as somewhere at the back of my mind I always feel the audience wants my blood.

The Vortex ends in tragedy, so the moment the comedy was over and the curtain went up on the third act, I happily galloped home like a horse to its stable.

It was while playing in *The Vortex* that I learned something about myself. I have never liked curtain calls at the end of a play—I mean when I am in it myself. But my dislike became a phobia in *The Vortex*. I really hated it when we had to go back on the stage after the last tragic scene, bowing to the audience with smiles on our faces.

What I have said will make a few people angry, I know. "Why shouldn't actors be applauded?" they will say. But equally, why should they be? We are doing a job that luckily for us is out of the rut, unlike many other jobs in life. I can only answer for myself, but this bowing embarrasses me. Some of the directors nowadays manage very cleverly to get around all this by *staging* the curtain calls, like the last, memorable production of *Love's Labour's Lost* at Stratford.

The Vortex was my last play on the stage. I have been offered some marvelous parts since then, but even if they want me in the future, I will never return. Never? It's not really my decision. I love going to a play and sitting in the audience, but I can't be on the other side of the footlights anymore. I wonder why?

My godson, Nicholas Daubeny, and I have always been very close. Ever since he was seven years old we have been able to talk about anything together, and discuss this world, the next and beyond! Although Nicholas has a marvelous brain, I think he agrees with me that beyond

knowledge there is "wisdom—the ability to have ac-
knowledged that which is bigger than oneself."

It is good for me to hear what someone still in his
twenties feels and believes in. We are both Aquarians and
so are more than interested in the New Age.

Nicholas took me a few years ago to see the Noh
Players when his father, Sir Peter Daubeny, brought
them over from Japan in his World Theatre program.
Nicky had seen them before, but he was fascinated to see
what effect they would have on me. From the moment
the curtain went up I sat entranced, though I could
hardly follow anything that was happening in their slow
movements so full of hidden meaning, but it didn't
matter. There seemed to be some strange inner feeling
that was holding us all together in the audience apart
from the stage, as if we were looking at them with the
Inner or Third Eye.

After the play was over Nicky took me back stage and
introduced me to the Players' manager and interpreter. I
asked him to explain the inner strength and discipline
that came over the footlights and I will always remember
his answer. "Before the curtain rises for the performance
they sit behind the curtain on stage in meditation and
prayer, thanking God for the gift that has been given
them, and with humility pray that they can pass on this
gift to the audience." They had no curtain calls at the
finish of the play, though the players clapped for the
audience at the end.

He continued: "I think the time has come now for
artists to go back and start again to work as Leonardo da
Vinci and Michelangelo did, with strict dedication to the
Creator who gave them the gift, and to consider themselves lucky beyond all measure and to acknowledge this.

The work of the artist has now so often become money. It must be changed back and dedication put in its place."

I often wonder what it is that makes me start on one of my films. I don't know the answer. The idea seems to come out of the blue and, if it is in the pattern of things, from then on it clicks and everything goes quite quickly as long as I grab and hold it, before it flies away on the wind.

I always love going to the British Museum and often spend nearly a whole day there when I have the time or I need references for my films. But on one particular day I felt an intense urgency to go there.

I happened to be passing through the Egyptian section when I suddenly caught the eye of the Pharaoh Rameses II. It really did seem like that, as he gazed down at me, so I sat on the bench facing him and began to think about my third film for the series.

What enormous and rather frightening statues they are. I tried to imagine what they must have looked like in their right surroundings under an Egyptian sky by the waters of the Nile. Then I began to get an idea for a film:

An Egyptian boy, locked in by mistake one night in the British Museum, has a dream about returning home. He steps into one of the upright sarcophaguses shaped like a figure, and with the brilliantly colored paintings and hieroglyphics inside and shuts himself in. In the dark he presses the black panel with his hands, and it swings around like *Alice Through the Looking Glass;* then in slow motion and with music getting louder and louder he finds himself in one of the tombs in Egypt, with the same paintings and hieroglyphics, and steps out into the brilliant sunshine of the desert of the Valley of the Kings.

Then he guides us through his country at its greatest period in history. . . .

I was still thinking about it when one of the attendants of the museum came up and told me to hurry as the bell had rung and they were closing. I nearly got locked in myself, which I wouldn't have cared for at all—however attractive Rameses II is.

I went back home and sat up all night reading and making notes about that glorious dynasty. By breakfast time I had decided that we should introduce Tutankhamen in the film as a boy in one scene and by "dissolving through" on the camera I could make the modern Egyptian boy become the pharaoh. Over this I could describe in my narration the frightening initiations he would have to have gone through at the temple of Karnak at Luxor.

I began to get very excited and went back to the British Museum to get advice from what I call one of their "old young men," who are hidden behind locked doors and are so full of knowledge and wisdom. He helped me to decide a lot about where and what we should film and insisted that we must go to Tell-el-Amana on the Nile which had nothing to show but a great evocative atmosphere. I was so grateful to him later on for having been firm about this. Naturally the producer argued that on a small budget we shouldn't waste our time there. I know nothing about the money side of these films, but I felt it was important that we go there, after filming the Temple of Abydos which was dark and menacing, and Dendera where Antony wooed Cleopatra.

Tell-el-Amana is now a ghost city, but three thousand years ago it was the glorious "City of Light" that the Pharaoh Akhenaton created for the One God, the new

religion and teaching that resembled Jesus Christ's fourteen hundred years later. "The City of Light" was
destroyed—razed to the ground by the priests—and
because Akhenaton was a man born before his time, he
was murdered, and they returned to the worship of their
old gods. I think I fell in love with Akhenaton and I
was determined that the film should be mostly about him
and his creative taste for beautiful free expression and
movement in paintings which seemed so modern. In the
tombs of his creation everything depicts light, in contrast
to the darkness of the pharaohs before him. He believed
in the One God for all—the deity behind the sun and
not in the sun itself—and some of the engravings show
the rays of the sun stretching down, pictured as hands
caressing the people. When I saw his statue for the first
time in the Cairo Museum—that strange misshapen
body, elongated artistic face, beautiful sensuous mouth
and the sensitive hands—I wanted to go down on my
knees and kiss these hands. My feeling of "knowing him"
was overwhelming—and perhaps I did? But he was
married to the beautiful Nefertiti!

I started things moving in the usual way to get an
invitation to go to Egypt as their guest. The government
was interested and arrangements were made for me to go
there. Soon after my arrival in Egypt I met President
Nasser by chance at a reception, which of course helped.
He asked me if I would film the Hilton Hotel in Cairo, to
put in my documentary. I tried to explain that my story
was about Egypt in all its past glory (that didn't go down
too well), and that the Hilton would look rather out of
place. I said: "When tourists come to London, sir, they
don't want to look at the Savoy Hotel or anything modern,
but the Beefeaters at the Tower of London."

He answered: "But everyone knows London has *got*

the Hilton, no one knows Cairo has it. We are proud of it and want it known."

We did not film the Hilton—it was never mentioned again.

Letters were then sent backward and forward by the producer through the embassies. I paid calls on the ambassadors in England after showing some of my films in London so that they could see the style of the series; eventually I arrived in Cairo.

Because I travel alone and am put up in glamorous hotels and a lot of fuss is made of me, it's always a letdown when everyone leaves me alone at end of the day. Sometimes, of course, I am given a fascinating gentleman to escort me everywhere and give me dinner off silver plates by candlelight, as I was last year in Israel; or as in Moscow, where a tall dashing Cossack arrived every morning before breakfast and sat on my unmade bed and drank his coffee and ate his bun with me before we set forth. But there are moments when I feel terribly alone. It happened in Cairo before I was joined by the unit and dear Johnnie (who had filmed my Greek picture the year before). I sat on the balcony of my suite in the hotel in my dressing down and stared at the Nile. The coloring of the sky was unbelievable—a scarlet-purple streaked by a bold artist's hand with emerald green straight across the heavens. Below were the *feluccas*, the ancient boats of the Nile, with their curved sails, sleepily floating on the calm waters of the river. I cried, of course, not because I was alone, but because I couldn't share this experience— no one is interested in what you have felt when you get home. The weight of Egypt and her age, which is fathomless, surround one and to think of trying to achieve anything new seems just a conceit and a waste of time.

When I am left alone like this I become a terrible flop in my own eyes and feel lost. I always imagine someone like Melina Mercouri in the same situation, dressed in a flowing robe, ringing bells, summoning waiters, telephoning the many friends one feels she must have whenever she steps out of a plane, dashing out to dinner—the jet set. I truly find it difficult even to get my meal sent up on a tray and never know what to do with myself between 7 P.M. and 10:30 P.M. except curl up in bed and go to sleep.

The moment the unit arrived, the "Curse of the Pharaohs" descended on us—and stayed off and on till we left Egypt. Then it took it up again in London. The most extraordinary but simple things went wrong, far beyond the usual trials and agonies of filming abroad in a strange country. It started with air pressure failing in the plane to Luxor; the oxygen masks didn't work and we were like fish out of water and it was freezing cold. I remember trying to move a piece of paper under my nose to create a little air to be able to breathe. We were lucky in that we were near Luxor or the plane would have landed with a lot of corpses, and also in that the pilot was not affected too badly. Of course there was no possibility of a forced landing as there was only desert below.

When we landed at Luxor the stewardess gathered enough breath to whisper to me, "Put your scarf over your face immediately or the skin will peel right off." So then from icy cold we were plunged into 110 degrees of blinding heat as she opened the door.

It was only the beginning of our troubles. Later in the day we were shooting scenes on the other side of the Nile in the Valley of the Kings, sometimes called the Valley of the Dead. No one is allowed to sleep there at night except the guardians of the tombs and their families so you have

to leave at sunset. Instead of returning on the public
ferry, we had hired a *felucca* so that we could film in our
own time and on our return try to catch the fairy-tale
colors of the sky. We got to the middle of the Nile when
Johnnie, who is one of the most particular and disciplined
people I have ever met on the job, informed us that even
though he had checked over and over again before we left
the Valley of the Dead, the most important part of the
camera was missing. In a panic we tried to hurry up the
felucca (which is impossible) to go back before dark and
find it, hoping we would be allowed to land. There was
still time to catch the last streaks of the sunset. We
landed—and hunted everywhere for this precious bit of
equipment. Johnnie had already searched his pockets
where he keeps a replacement. That had disappeared too.
We returned to Luxor without filming.

The next day, after Johnnie had found the replacement
in a most unexpected place, we started off again. The
same thing happened—an exact repetition, but this time
the boat stuck as well and wouldn't move, although
people pushed and shoved with oars. After that we tied
the "precious bit" around his neck and took the public
ferry, and all felt more secure.

Another time we were filming Pharaoh Seti I's tomb—
the deepest one of all. It was extremely hot down there
and to me very claustrophobic and eerie with all the
figures stiffly painted on the walls fixing us with their
expressionless stares. I found the whole atmosphere
frightening and oppressive. I asked if I could go up above
and get some air while the camera was set up for my
close-up. I climbed out of the tomb and strolled only a few
hundred yards into the desert, took a few big breaths, and
then turned around to go back—I was lost. I could see
nothing but just miles and miles of sand. I have been in

many deserts these last few years, and whereas I used to find the solitude and emptiness overpowering, I have learned that if you can take the desert and fill the void yourself, you are achieving something even greater than that which the mountains can give you with their height and isolation. But this time I got into a real panic and did the worst thing I could have done. I turned around and around, looking everywhere, and lost all bearings. I realized later, of course, that if I had stood quite still, they would have come to look for me.

Seti I is not one of my favorite pharaohs and I began to feel he wasn't liking the idea of our poking around in his tomb. A slight wind got up. I started to whistle. The film unit knew I loved to be alone sometimes and were obviously not worrying. I began to shout—at last, someone appeared above ground and was very surprised at the state I was in. We went down below again and filmed, those static figures on the walls staring at us, so different from the lively dancing girls of Akhenaton's era. I was quite relieved when we finished and were about to come up for air. The focus boy went up first carrying the camera. He was large and strong. He had to be as he sometimes coped with heavy equipment. I came out next. As I started up the rickety staircase, I heard him call out from the top. He was lying on the ground and said he suddenly felt ill and found difficulty in breathing. I told him to lie still and that I was coming. Halfway up the stairs, I couldn't put one foot in front of the other. I was "locked," and then frighteningly I felt my arms being pulled backward and then my body pulled back into the tomb. I wrenched my body forward. It happened again, but I was able to break it and crawl up to join the boy at the top.

Next Johnnie came out. Oblivious to what had happened to us, he shouted up to me: "I can't make the stairs, Ann. What's the matter with me? I can't get up." He had quite a struggle. The rest of the unit, except for feeling terribly tired, had no trouble, perhaps because they all came up together. I don't know, but we three experienced something strange all right, and I was glad to say goodbye to Seti I.

It is well known that the pharaohs had knowledge of many mysteries of life and death that we know nothing about. The act of leaving the body was one of them. There are people who believe that many of them are still on earth in spirit, their bodies in trance. If this is true I can understand why the most powerful dynasty that existed does not appreciate the way modern man has opened up their tombs of peace and, what I think is most revolting, laid them out like corpses in the mummy room of the Cairo Museum. It made me feel quite sick to see those beautiful powerful proud kings and queens degraded to skulls and bones. I would understand their fury at the mutilation of their bodies if they wished to return to them—so I can well believe in the Curse of the Pharaohs.

When we returned to England we had one scene to film at night in the British Museum. We had brought the Egyptian boy back with us. First he didn't like the mummy room in the museum, and we had trouble getting him to walk through it. In the end we filmed without him. This may only have been because of his upbringing, but then the guard dogs didn't like the idea either and behaved very strangely. At last, before we left, we took a close-up of Rameses II looking down on me and the reverse angle of my close-up looking up at him. Then we packed up for the night. Next day the laboratory telephoned to say my close-up was ruined. There was a half-inch blue streak straight down the middle of my face. The cameras were checked and everything was gone into. Nothing was wrong, but we had to go back again to the museum, which cost money, and repeat the shot. Next day the same report came in. After that we went straight to the studio and cheated my close-up away from Rameses!

We had one last experience when we were recording my voice for narration and mixing in the music and sound effects. This is always tricky, and I greatly admire the skill of the people who carry it out. Apart from the detailed mechanics of the operation and the different volumes to be controlled for music and speech, it needs an artist with a sensitive understanding to pull it off in very little space of time, and to please everyone, not least the actor or actress who wants all the subtleties of the light and shade of the performance to be preserved. Jock is such a man—a great character, who always wears a kilt. He has done most of my films and I always like working with him very much.

This time all was going well till we started on the Valley of the Kings; then, each time my narration, already recorded, got to the description of the dead, the sound stopped and the screen broke down. We spent a precious hour trying to get it but failed. At last Johnnie looked at me and said: "From one Celt to another, I think you had better leave the studio; we will do better without you around perhaps." He laughed. I think he meant it as a joke—but I went—and they got it.

We must have won in the end, because it turned out to be a film of great beauty. The audiences often used to applaud at the end. Once I happened to be there. It was a funny feeling—sitting at the back of the cinema, not recognized, and hearing them clap—but for an actress nice, definitely nice.

The opening of the film *Thunder of the Kings* is so spectacular that it has been written about quite a lot, thanks to Johnnie. I asked him before we went to Egypt if he could make the three great pyramids "grow up" out of the sand like phallic symbols to thunderous music. Johnnie said the trick photography would be too difficult, but he never says no for long and one dawn our small unit collected together facing the giants. We all shoveled away the sand to make a hole in which to sink the camera. It was maddening how the sand trickled back through our fingers, but whatever Johnnie did, it worked in the end, with all our efforts. The pyramids rose up into an Egyptian sky and as the Sphinx says when he speaks during the *son et lumière* performance in Cairo:

I saw Antony and Cleopatra pass
Alexander, Caesar and Napoleon paused at my feet
I saw the ambitious dreams of Conquerors
Whirling like dead leaves
As my motto I chose an Arab saying
The World fears Time—but Time fears the Pyramids.

CHAPTER 12

A Persian Fairy Tale

After the Rank Organisation took over the distribution of my film series, everything went much more smoothly, thanks to Frank Poole, who was managing director until recently. He had stipulated that my name should appear above the titles, so they are shown as Ann Todd's *Thunder in Heaven,* and so on, for world distribution.

When I first started the series I used to be able to act from time to time in other films or television. This was while the producer was engaging the unit, fixing up contracts, and so on, but after the fourth film of my series I found it more and more demanding and difficult to find the time to do other things, though I clung to the saying, "Things that are difficult take time; things that are impossible take a little longer." Ingrid and I often send a telegram quoting this to each other when facing some chaotic crisis.

Very soon after I returned from Egypt I was at a dinner party given by one of the young Roosevelts. It was to be a large and rather grand affair, mostly diplomatic people and ambassadors, and of course Americans. I very nearly didn't go, but I am glad I did as it turned out to be my destiny again.

I had a vivacious American sitting on my right who chatted me up and made me laugh. Then I realized I was being rude to the gentleman on my left. He was a foreigner, very attractive but silent, and he wore dark glasses, which make it difficult to contact people in bright sun and impossible at night by candlelight. I turned to the American on my right and whispered: "I haven't got my glasses and I can't read his name on the place card. Could you lean over me and look?"

Just as he bent forward the gentleman on my left put his wine glass down on the card, quite by accident, but that was that. I turned to him again, trying to make conversation, when he suddenly said: "I don't think you have made a film of my country, have you? Do you know it?" I lost my head—dinner was nearly over. I had been a bit rude and he was obviously someone I should have known.

I stammered, "No, no—yes, oh! that would be very interesting," and prayed it wasn't Nepal, Greece or Egypt.

He then changed the subject rather disconcertingly and said in French, "I like your smile."

I brightened up and answered, "That's strange, a taxi driver told me last week it made him cry."

The ladies were then ushered upstairs. I rushed over to the one female I knew and asked who he was. "The Persian ambassador," she said. The moment the men joined us I pounced on the surprised ambassador and told him how I would love to make a film of his country.

A few days later a library of books arrived from the

Iranian Embassy on Cyrus the Great, the Shah, etcetera. Soon after a very chic French lady was brought to tea by a friend of mind. As she got up to go, she glanced at my large pile of enormous books and said: "You are interested in Persia?"

I said, "Oh, yes," then showing off, I added: "These were sent round by the ambassador."

As she went to the door she threw over her shoulder: "Oh, *I* got earrings from Aspreys."

I am sure His Excellency, if he should read this, won't mind and will be amused, as I later became a friend of his. I have a sneaking feeling that the French lady was trying to upstage me. She didn't succeed.

Two years later I was in Persia. I like that name so much better than Iran. It seems tragic what is going on now in that country. I never saw the unhappy, perhaps ugly, things that may have been happening then. I didn't see them perhaps because my story after all was a fairy tale. For myself, a dozen years ago, I found only dignity and beauty.

On the night I arrived in Tehran I was bidden to a big diplomatic reception and dinner, which were to be held at the spectacular and famous Gulistan Palace. This time I was the guest of the Foreign Office, who later backed my film. As usual I was alone on this first visit. My host had been the ambassador in London and was now foreign secretary. Everyone was very dressed up. The men wore orders and medals. There were footmen in uniform at the entrance of the palace and, as I got out of the car they had sent for me, I felt I was really playing *Cinderella*—a sort of dream. I was wearing a long floating mauve-and-pink chiffon dress embroidered here and there in gold and a feather boa dyed to match that reached to the floor. As I mounted the red-carpeted stairs under the gigantic chandeliers flickering all the colors of the universe, I saw myself in the famous mirrors on either side—me—reflected over and over again. It all looked like a pretty fantastic set for a film. I wanted to giggle when I realized that I had never even walked on a stage looking like this. I was acting, or rather over-acting, a part that I had never played before. I swept on and was announced to the foreign secretary.

After the reception there was a long dinner with lots of speeches in Arabic and Persian *and* the translations! I sat between a Spaniard and a Persian, and conversation was by signs. Then we all adjourned to an enormous room and stood drinking our coffee. No one spoke to me. I began to feel very hot. I went up to the kindest looking face and asked her if she thought I could go. She said, "Definitely no. None of the ambassadors has left yet." I hung around till a white-haired, distinguished-looking gentleman wearing a colored sash said goodbye to our host, then I sprinted up to him.

As he spoke to me in French I thought I would boldly answer in my French. *"Je vous remercie infinement, votre excellence, pour une très, très bonne nuit,"* I said.

My host smiled, held my hand and answered, *"Soirée,* yes?"

I always think the French language is full of dangers.

My story for the film was about four Persian children, two boys and two girls, welcoming me to Tehran. By looking into a fountain and wishing, we all went back in time and found ourselves wearing the Persian trousers and beautiful transparent coats that are found in the famous miniatures. The children were then to take me on a journey visiting Shiraz, Isfahan and Persepolis, that great city of the past in the desert.

After everything was fixed up I returned to London and gathered my unit together.

When all was settled and the unit ready, I went back to Tehran and found that in my absence an audience had been arranged to present me to the empress. She is a fascinating person, casually chic, and in a charming way she puts one at one's ease. We were talking about my fairy story when she suddenly said, "Would you like my son to play in the last scene as the prince when he meets all the children? My husband and I would give permission."

I longed to answer, "Oh, no, no, please don't offer him to us, it will make everything even more difficult and I can't cope." But I quickly realized what she had said and answered, "I don't know what to say, Your Majesty—you must know what it would mean to me and the film. Yes, please."

She then said, "He is being a little difficult at the moment." (He was about eight years old.) "What would you like him to wear? He prefers shorts and a blazer—but what would you like?" I didn't mind what he wore if we had him, but I suggested long trousers, as I thought he would look rather touching walking up to the Peacock Throne. The empress said that they would try to get him into them.

The day arrived for filming His Royal Highness. I was shaking with nerves. We arrived at 8 A.M. at the Gulistan Palace. Our cameras and equipment were stripped and searched. Everyone except the cameraman, our manager and myself was sent away—then one of our light bulbs blew up and the armed guards jumpe to attention. They advanced on me when I opened my powder compact to powder my nose. The heat was terrible, no air conditioning, and I had to wear a hat and gloves. At 10 A.M.

we got a message that the prince was leaving the palace outside Tehran; all roads were closed and police were lining the approach. I couldn't take it in. I had written a short synopsis, met the empress, and had been offered the heir to the throne for my half-hour film—it all seemed incredible.

The car arrived at great speed. We could hear the sentries saluting and then people mounting the stairs. They entered—a small charming little boy came in with the most wonderful smile in the world, wearing long trousers. Behind him were three ministers, the lord chamberlain, armed bodyguards and Mademoiselle Joyeux, his governess. I did my bob but longed to hug him for the trousers! I made a speech of three lines thanking him for the honor and introduced him to the cameraman. Then I asked the governess if she spoke English. "No," she answered. I asked her then in my brave French if I could tell the people around the prince to *sortir?*"

"No," she said and added, "He is very nervous,"

I thought, "Not as much as me." The prince spoke only Persian or French. I explained to him that we wanted him to walk up the red carpet onto a certain mark on the floor, turn and give us his terrific smile (while we zoomed in to a large close-up, filling the screen for the ending of my fairy tale); and then we would see his small figure retreating toward his father's throne.

We had one tricky moment when I asked the prince to repeat the scene. He was jumping up and down and saying, *"Je suis un acteur,"* and we were all clapping and saying, "Bravo," when he suddenly stopped, drew himself up, waved his hands regally and said *"non"* firmly. We had to have a second take to cover ourselves on such an important scoop.

I pleaded: *"Votre Altesse, encore une fois, je vous en prie."*

"Non," answered the heir to the throne. No one moved. Then Mademoiselle Joyeux approached him and whispered something in Persian in his ear. I would love to have known what it was. "You will be walloped by Father"? "You won't get any ice cream"? or what? But like an angel he came up to me and, with that smile that surely melts anyone who meets him, said in a loud voice, *"Oui, Madame."*

The last I saw of him, His Royal Highness was sitting on his own throne sucking Coca-Cola through a straw.

The unit and I went to an extremely expensive restaurant for lunch and had lots to drink and no more work for the day.

After the glamor and nerves of the day at the palace with the prince, we settled down to more ordinary scenes, if anything could be called ordinary in Persia. We had to film a reverse shot to show what the prince was smiling at on the screen. The palace wouldn't allow him to be shot (we had terrible trouble with that word in all countries and all languages) with the other children in the film, so now we had to film two hundred children all under eleven years old representing the children of the world. I persuaded the embassies to send children dressed in the costumes of their countries. The Japanese child was only four and looked adorable in her kimono and her hair piled up with flowers and ivory pins. I also used some children from the local orphanage and put them in front. We made them all enter the palace as quietly as possible, just whispering as they crept up the stairs, then stopping breathless with excitement as they entered the Peacock Throne room and saw the prince smiling back.

The four children who played all through the film with

me, Azita, 9, Ramine, 6, Ferozande, 11, and Mahomed, 12, were delightful. Two of them were embassy children and two were from the orphanage. Only Ramine, the youngest, spoke French, and he of course, was the wickedest. I had to ask him sometimes in French to give a message to the others if the interpreter was busy. I never knew what he said but it was always followed by giggles.

When we had finished filming various scenes in Tehran we were scheduled to fly to Isfahan to continue filming the story, which was about the children's search for the sun that had been stolen and so had plunged the world into darkness. Before I was allowed to fly the little orphans out of Tehran I had to visit the guardians of the orphanage. I found myself facing two ladies wearing the *chador,* with faces completely hidden except for black eyes staring at me. We sat in silence. I felt as if they were almost boring a hole through me as they summed me up. Then they gave their permission. I presumed they trusted me.

Our flight to Isfahan lasted two hours. The children had never flown before and they skipped excitedly up and down in the plane. Their chaperone was sick. I went over to her just before we landed at Isfahan and asked if I could help her. She was heavily veiled. She said no. It was only just that she was pregnant and the baby was due, she thought, any minute. We had her off the plane and onto another back to Tehran before we left the airport!

We started filming the moment we arrived. The mosques with their gigantic domes looked like something out of the *Arabian Nights,* and the women dressed all in black—covered completely—were like silent crows wandering in and out of them for their moments of prayer. I had to enter one of the mosques to discuss where we should place our cameras for the scene we were about to shoot. All women must be veiled before they can enter, so I was forced to wear the *chador.* Clutching my large handbag and my shoes—which had to come off—underneath it and covering my face and head with the cloth, held in position between my teeth, to keep me masked, was quite a feat.

That evening we had our first night shooting with the children in the hotel, which was the world-famous Shah Abbas Hotel. It is quite fantastic with its Eastern opulence, and we all felt for the first time that this was really Persia! We were filming in a magnificent courtyard and garden surrounded by mosaics and fabulous carpets hanging on the walls. There were hundreds of small Persian fairy lamps like those in *Aladdin,* swinging in the soft breeze. In the middle of the court was a fountain and there was music in the background. The smell of jasmine and those magic domes with the colors of blue, green and gold that one sees in a child's fairy story book dominated it all. The stars were so low they seemed to be touching the mosaics and the Persian moon was lying on its back. It all looked exactly like a set—one that we couldn't afford nowadays—for an epic Hollywood film, and I had chosen it, this magic place, on my first visit to Persia. I was thrilled to get a pat on the back from my camera director.

The filming was going well, the children were very excited and, with a lot of laughter, we had just finished filming a scene where we were floating around this fairy garden in our Persian clothes, when suddenly, at 2:30 A.M., I got into a panic. We had lost one of the little girls, Ferozande, who looked older than eleven. I made the others curl up on the sofa in the hall of the hotel and searched for her. I found her hand in hand with a gentleman of around fifty, strolling along the corridors. I don't know what he thought, but I snatched her from him, glared at him as if he had raped her, got very cross, out of fright, with Ferozande, who didn't understand a word, and hauled her back to the others. I then went off to do my close-up with a crumpled anxious face, asking the cameraman to hurry, hurry, please. When I returned to the children, Ramine had gone. I found him in the gentleman's loo playing with the taps. I took no notice of the gentlemen in there and, throwing French words at Ramine which I didn't know I knew, I dragged him out. After that no more night shooting for the children and few close-ups of me.

From then on I was left to cope with four healthy mischievous children and to act in the film. I used to iron their film clothes before filming each morning, see they went to the loo and ate their food, play with them, put them to bed and hear their prayers to Allah. Ramine, one night, flung his arms round my neck and hugged me. I sang him to sleep as if he were one of my grandchildren, and just before he went off, he turned his head away and said sleepily, "*Bonsoir, Maman.*"

We were three days working in Isfahan, then we all flew to Shiraz. While waiting at the airport for our plane we saw a delicious scene enacted. A woman, obviously very rich and wearing a mask of heavy cloth and black leather over her nose and eyes, was sitting on the floor enveloped in her *chador*. On the chair, where she should have been sitting, sat smugly her cheap handbag made of plastic. She stared adoringly at it and kept polishing and stroking this common object, which somehow took on a supercilious look. The men in the party were magnificently attired with jeweled belts. They looked rich and distinguished and seemed to be covered with gold.

When the plane at last arrived and we were asked to embark, the husband snapped his fingers at the lady on the floor and she and her bag rose up to follow him. Her *chador* parted for a moment and under it I saw she was wearing a very daring miniskirt, well above her knees. She had high-heeled French shoes and very sheer silk stockings. I was told the outer garment is removed when at home. I suppose it is hung up in the hall, like our raincoats. I don't know where the bag goes!

We arrived late at Shiraz; the sunset was spectacular, and the children overexcited and out of control. This place is called "the City of Roses and Nightingales" and is also well-known for its poets. The most famous of these are Hafiz and Saadi. I loved it. To me it was the friendliest spot in Persia. Even the famous roses and tall stately cypress trees seemed to welcome us, with their inner calmness and peace.

We stayed four days here on the edge of the desert, and I became very worried at one moment as Ramine, our youngest child in the film, looked as if he had measles, or whatever is the equivalent in Persia. The unit was marvelous, as they always seem to be with children. We put him to bed and starved him for a day, and all the spots disappeared, but at that moment I longed for the chaperone, pregnant or not pregnant.

After Shiraz, we drove in our jeeps and Land-Rover, to Persepolis—that fabulous city in the middle of the desert. Around 450 B.C. emperors from India, Africa and Ethiopia, princes from Arabia, and men from Mecca and Egypt all came here with their gifts, traveling on camels and horseback across the desert to give and share their wisdom. It must have been a stupendous sight. Such elegance: palaces with their black and gray pillars, doors of gold, furniture of sandalwood and ebony, and colored ceramics on the walls. Persepolis had majesty and splendor. I felt great power there and a commanding force strong enough to evoke that power.

There was a storm the night we arrived. At first we thought we would have to give up as it would be impossible to film the children. However, I decided to go ahead alone; it was very effective, as I walked through the deserted city with the fierce wind blowing my Persian dress and the stormy sky above. It was very original done this way and, I think, it turned out pretty good.

The film was shown under the title *A Persian Fairy Tale* and was out on release for a second time; I wonder if that will be the last time it will be seen? Yes, probably for a long, long time. I must remember to leave it in my will to my son and daughter as a relic of the past.

Persia is summed up for me by Shakespeare's words in *The Tempest*:

> Our revels now are ended. These our actors,
> As I foretold you, were all spirits, and
> Are melted into air, into thin air:
> And, like the baseless fabric of this vision,
> The cloud-capp'd towers, the gorgeous palaces,
> The solemn temples, the great globe itself,
> Yea, all which it inherit, shall dissolve,
> And, like the insubstantial pageant faded,
> Leave not a rack behind. We are such stuff
> As dreams are made on, and our little life
> Is rounded with a sleep.

CHAPTER 13

Thunder of Silence

"I t is difficult in our world today to find silence and 'take it' because it means being stripped down into a void to face the truth and find out what one really is, without the trimmings."

When I read that short statement in the *Daily Mail*, quoting a remark of King Hussein, it gave me the idea of making my next film in the Hashimite Kingdom, in the desert.

I contacted the Jordanian ambassador in London, who was very helpful, and he arranged that I should visit his country as their guest and have an audience with His Majesty, so in 1975 I flew off alone to get permission and the backing for filming. On arrival I was given a guide-interpreter to look after me, and on the second day I was driven out into the desert around Amman. We had just passed the Hunting Lodges with their sauna baths, dated

A.D. 716, when we were hit by the most frightening
sandstorm. It was impossible to drive, as one couldn't see
anything, so we just sat there with the windows tightly
shut. The heat was so great that I thought I was going to
pass out. Later I opened one window just a slit to be able
to breathe, and the sand immediately covered our eyes
and hair and clogged our noses. I don't know how long
we remained there, but wave after wave of sand, like a
fierce rough sea, rolled over us accompanied by a high
whistling wind.

The moment the storm subsided, which it did as
suddenly as it had started, we drove back to Amman.

I plunged into a bath and put my head under the water.
Then the telephone rang. It was the palace informing me
that my audience with King Hussein was that afternoon;
I would be called for in one and a half hours. Panic. I
struggled with my matted hair. All the shops were closed.
But when my hair was finally clean, the sun had left the
balcony of my suite and I had no hair dryer and no hat. I
rubbed my head with a towel, then sat bolt upright in a
chair and called on Allah for help. It came. The palace
rang after an hour to say that my audience was canceled
till the next day.

Next morning I was taken to the *souk*, the mar-
ketplace, where I hopefully bought one of their beautiful
necklaces to wear when the film was made. I have always
believed that if you are certain something is going to
come off and "see" it materializing, it happens.

In the afternoon, all dressed up, I went to the palace.

On either side of the entrance stood the sentries, the
tallest men I have ever seen—like Cossacks, in their high
fur hats . . . and in that heat too. I was taken to the
waiting room and sat there with many others for half an
hour. Then I was summoned. My turn came after that of

a sheik, a Bedouin from the desert, who had asked only to be in the king's presence for a second or two.

His Majesty came to the door to receive me. I did my bob, then quite informally he led me to a sofa. He had seen me at the Old Vic as Lady Macbeth and said how happy he was to meet me and made other kind comments. I interrupted him and said, "Your Majesty, you are saying all the things I had prepared to say to you."

The king of Jordan is an extremely hard-working monarch—and most days, if their requests are genuine, he sees some of his subjects to give advice and hear their complaints. He was dressed in a black shirt, sleeves rolled up, open collar and light-colored trousers. He apologized for his appearance. I thought he looked terribly tired, but when I remarked, before I left, how exhausted I thought he must get, he smiled that marvelous smile, so well-known, and said, "Not if I can help people," and added, "Solomon managed!" He said he would help me over the film, and that he liked the synopsis, though he had forgotten the words he had said which had first struck me in the *Daily Mail* until I produced a copy.

It was difficult to realize that his life was in constant danger. I was told that someone had even tried to kill him by poisoning his toothpaste and his nose drops, and several cats had been found dead in the palace grounds. It was presumed a poison was being tested.

The king honored me before I left by giving me the Hashimite Star, the highest order of Jordan, which is given for courage. I wrote him a letter ending, "It is such an honor, Your Majesty, to be given the Hashimite Star, but even more so because it has been given by someone who represents *courage* to the world more than anyone else."

I was to travel many miles by jeep or Land-Rover with

my guide who interpreted for me. He called me Missie Ann.

What a wonderful moment it was as we crossed the desert to see, like a mirage in the distance, Azraz, and that cool green oasis surrounded by trees. Thousands of birds migrating across the world meet there, and as I said in my film later it is where "peace is stronger than hate." Lawrence of Arabia used to go there to meditate.

One day I was taken into the house of the old man who guards Lawrence's Fort, and he insisted on dressing me up as one of the women of the Druze Tribe. He gave me a long red skirt, embroidered apron, short velvet waistcoat, rounded hat and veil. I sat on the floor with him, in silence. We just smiled at each other and nodded now and again as we drank our coffee and absorbed the peace. It was hard to leave.

Then we continued our journey across the desert. Camels and their young galloped beside us, their strange throat cries echoing in the silence, until we came to the outpost of the Desert Police—who never see any women till they go on leave. Their fort was very high up as a lookout, with the most spectacular view in every direction.

When we arrived I was exhausted after the drive and the heat, so I asked if I could lie down. I was taken into a long room with several beds and sank down onto one of them as hard as a board and fell asleep before my head touched the rock that was the pillow. I woke up two hours later and to my surprise found myself surrounded by gentlemen snoring away on either side of me.

We drank together the many cups of strong black coffee that are always offered; it would be very impolite to refuse. The ritual is to accept two cups, then shake the cup from side to side and refuse the third. I was being asked lots of questions through the interpreter, when a solemn handsome Arab who had stared at me during all the laughter at my attempts to try out my Arabic, spoke to the interpreter without taking his eyes off me. We waited; then the interpreter said, "The sheik wants to know how old you are."

I suddenly felt very womanly and wondered how many camels I was worth before he bought me. I answered, bowing to him, "Sadly, sir, much too old for you; thank you for the honor."

Later, as we were driving the two hundred and fifty miles through the desert back to Amman, the guide said, "Missie Ann, was it wrong for the sheik to have said that to you?"

I said, "Well, no, but it is not done *often* in the West. I think if he had asked it in France, though, he might have had his face slapped."

"Oh, Missie Ann, I *am* so relieved you didn't do that," he said. "You would have been knifed." He looked really shaken.

On our way to Wadi Rhum we stopped for one night at a tiny place in the desert with welcome palm trees for shade. All the water had ceased, so there was no toilet working and no washing possible. In the night I woke up to see what looked like something out of a Disney film dancing on the floor at the end of my camp bed. "It" stood up, stretched its arms and legs out in the shaft of moonlight it happened to be in, turned its head sharply and looked at me.

I started to speak gently, as I do with wasps at home. "*Please* leave my room, I am sure you ought to be out of doors, it's much cooler there." It stood on its hind legs; then I shouted *"Yala"* which I felt it must understand as it means "Get out" in Arabic, and I repeated it three

With Ivan Desny in *Madeleine*.

Breaking Through the Sound Barrier.

Breaking Through the Sound Barrier with Sir Ralph Richardson and Nigel Patrick.

Left, David Lean and me, off to So Africa on tour with the *Comet—* plane that "starred" with me in *Bre ing Through the Sound Barrier; Abo* My son, David Malcolm, escorting for the first time to a film premier 1952.

Top left, as Lady Percy in *Henry IV Part II* at the Old Vic; *Top right*, as Katherina in *The Taming of the Shrew*; *Below*, With Paul Rogers in *The Taming of the Shrew*. CROWN COPYRIGHT, THEATRE MUSEUM, LONDON

As Lady Macbeth at the Old Vic.

Ingrid Bergman, me and Whisky on a shopping trip; *Below left*, Cookie and me sitting by the swimming pool of the Hollywood Chateau Marmont Hotel; *Below right*, In the television production of *Camille*, with David Knight as Armand.

THAMES TELEVISION

Below, at an art exhibition with Vivien
Leigh during the run of *Duel of Angels*.

Above right, with my daughter and two of my grandchildren, Oliver and
Florent; *Below left*, *Son of Captain Blood*. *Below right*, with Mme. Vijaya
Pandit Nehru at an Indian Embassy reception.

PARAMOUNT

With Gary Cooper just before he died.

Being entertained by the shiek in the Jordanian desert Wadi Rhum while filming *Thunder of Silence*.

With Nepalese students at Pashupatinath. I was amazed when
they asked me to recite a few
verses of Shakespeare.

Me today.

times. "It" paused, then in its own time sauntered off, head in the air. I piled everything I could find including my pillow and fur coat around where the door should have been and prayed it couldn't climb. At breakfast next morning I was told that it had been a large scorpion and, after visiting me, it had called on someone else.

Incidentally, our meals were interesting, as the man who cooked spoke only Italian and Arabic, my guide only Arabic and English, the Egyptian who ran the place Arabic and French, and I English and French. It was hilarious, but how I loved it, sitting all together around that large wooden table eating a kind of black bread and drinking those copious cups of coffee.

Then we arrived at Wadi Rhum—what a place! As the light faded and the mountains around the camp turned to rose pink, it was like being in another world. There were two tribes passing through with their camels, women and children. Long brown tents low to the ground against the wild desert wind. The head sheik of the Desert Legions had a large and grand tent where I used to go in the evenings to talk, through my guide, and drink coffee under the stars. The stars, so close that it seemed almost possible to put up a hand and pluck one out of that incredible midnight-blue sky. There was an old man full of wisdom who joined us. He was a hundred and fifteen years old but very spry; he had fought with Lawrence of Arabia.

The sheik had given me one of their black robes bordered with gold, called a *burnous*. So that night, wrapping this around me, I walked alone into the desert away from the tents and the singing and music of the Desert Legion, played on the violin-shaped instruments of the Bedouin tribes. In the complete and profound silence that enveloped me, I began to think again of the strength of

the universe that surrounds us. In the atmosphere of
pure strong air and light, found here in the desert, and in
the Himalayas or even on the beach in Suffolk, surely
there must be contained some great energy? And as the
universe and thought are energy, I felt maybe if one
could tune in correctly, like finding a program on the
radio, it might be possible to contact it. A kind of free-
flowing energy would then be opened to us to be used on
all levels. Because in proportion to one's *awareness* of the
presence of God, or the life force, so is the power of God
available—just as with electricity, which was always
present throughout the ages, but what benefit was it to
mankind? None, because there was no conscious realiza-
tion of its existence. It was there all the time and available
if they had only known how to utilize it. The power of the
universe is also there if we learn how to make use of it. As
I looked up that night at the silent serene moon, it
seemed to nod! But when I returned to the Desert Legion
and squatted again in their tent and listened to their
songs, I could feel their peace and I wondered if perhaps
after all the real answer was quite simply just innocence
and complete trust. Why complicate things?

The sheik asked me one night to describe our washing
machines in the West. He was fascinated and asked if
this machine gave us happiness! It was difficult to
answer him, as my happiness was sitting cross-legged in
his tent in the desert.

Once when no one was looking I went into the desert
alone again and stood where David Lean had collected
together all the trappings of a big feature film unit—
hundreds of people—for that suberb film he made of
Lawrence of Arabia on the very spot where I was
standing now. I stamped my foot and shouted to the sky,

"I can do it too," and I did. It was not quite the same though!

When we arrived at Wadi Rhum I was ill. The last hundred miles in the jeep was a bit of a nightmare. I had a high temperature and rather a bad pain in my side. They laid me down on a rug in my tent and sent for one of the sheiks. He knelt down beside me, looking exactly like an older Lawrence, and placed one of his hands on my forehead, the other on my stomach. After a moment or two of silence he said to my guide, "Tell the lady I will give her the desert herbs for the moment, till her mind is rested. Then of course her mind will take control again of her body and all will be well." Just this assumption that naturally my mind was strong enough to settle it all made me feel like a god—far better than a doctor's insistence that his pill would put it right. I was OK next morning. The sheik and my guide had come four times in the night with their herbs, and my temperature had shot down. If I hadn't recovered, it would have been tricky, as no plane could have landed and there was no radio or communication with Amman.

When we returned to this place later to film, I used to lay my clothes out with boulders to hold them down on the sand, and the fierce sun in the morning ironed them out for me; when traveling on these films we don't take a woman with us—it would be asking too much. Anyway, it's impossible with the heat, wind and cold to use make-up. When it's really tough I wear a wig exactly the same as my own hairstyle. I put it on like a hat, and I was the only member of our team in Nepal who didn't get sunstroke!

We left Wadi Rhum at dawn one morning and fifty men of the Desert Legion came to say goodbye and wish us well. It was a most exciting moment as they passed us in full gallop on their camels, shouting their war song and brandishing their rifles, rather like watching a performance of *The Desert Song*.

We got going at last, after many goodbyes, and started before the great heat of the day toward Petra—the "Rose Red City half as old as Time," the Eighth Wonder of the World.

The king was so determined that I should look good in the film that he ordered me a side saddle from England and suggested one of his Arab horses from the royal stables. I went as fast as I could to Petra and sat astride one of the gentle sleepy tourist horses. It was called Saloir, which means Joy. Thank goodness it didn't live up to its name.

When later I apologized to His Majesty for not accepting his offer because of my fear of horses, he said: "The horse couldn't have done much; the ravine is so narrow it could only walk forward or sit down."

The first impression of Petra (which means Rock) as one approaches it from the desert is the strangeness of the place. It's as if one has left behind all the known things of life and is experiencing the feelings of having wandered into another world. When one looks at the vast rocks confronting one, there seems to be no visible sign of an entrance.

As I say in my film: "Petra was the stronghold of the Nabataean Arab Kingdom from the second century B.C. to the third century A.D. The only opening is a narrow slit in the towering rocks, which made it possible for these tribes, using only a handful of men, to ransom the passing caravans on their way to Damascus and to hold up the great Roman army; but the wealthy city's only water supply came from outside its walls, so when their secret was known they became vulnerable and were then conquered by Rome."

Entering the *siq* (the ravine) for the first time was one of the most exciting sensations that I have ever experienced. Here is perpetual twilight, with just now and again a glint of sun, high above, where the rocks almost touch overhead, and below it is only just wide enough to ride or walk. There is no sound except the pebbles under the horses' hooves and the sighing of the wind. The music of Wagner went through my head and every time we turned a corner it was as if the Valkyries were calling me, on and on. (I used this music later over this scene when we made the film.) As we rode through the darkness, I had the feeling of dying—coming from darkness into light?—or of birth, having been in the womb? Either way, a rebirth.

Then suddenly, without any warning one is left dazed and bewildered at what one faces. I really couldn't believe my eyes. It was too dramatic, too unreal. There in front of us was the Rose-Red City—and *really* rose-red and pink and sensual, looking like a vast stage set, already lit for opera, to be sung by giants. Temples—tombs—palaces—theaters—houses—baths—superb staircases—all created and cut out of the living rocks. There were wild shapes, great elemental cleavages and brilliant rain-washed colors streaking down the rocks like falling rainbows. And complete silence. A secret city. No one there except some donkeys and goats, half a dozen people living in the caves and the guide and me.

It was very eerie. I felt that I had gone back in time and that I knew I had stood here before. I was rather glad to hear a cock crow suddenly—a fierce strong male note that echoed around the towering rocks that encircled us.

It was reassuring—and brought me sharply back to the 1970s.

Mr. Mustapha, my Arab guide-interpreter, was round, short and cuddly like a Teddy Bear. We had traveled together for many hundreds of miles through the desert and lonely places, but the moment we entered the Hidden City I noticed a very small change in his manner. I wanted to see the sunset and the dawn in this magic place, so arrangements had been made to stay the night at a so-called rest house, a kind of glorified hut outside Petra. No one is allowed to sleep within its walls. We would have to hurry because of the half hour it took riding back through the ravine. Before departing Mr. Mustapha and I sat down to drink some revolting coffee out of our thermos. He poured my cup and handed it to me. I raised my eyes and thanked him. Mr. Mustapha was not looking at me in the same way as he had done two hours earlier. There was quite a different expression in his eyes—his face was still round and kind, but there was a definite smirk on it. However hard I tried not to, I felt as if I were sitting on a rock in the Hidden City with no clothes on.

Mr. Mustapha said, "Would you care to explore Petra again—now—Missie Ann?"

I answered immediately in my most controlled Albert Hall student voice: "No, thank you, Mr. Mustapha. I am tired and anyway it's getting too dark to see."

"Don't worry," said Mr. Mustapha. "I know how you like to 'feel' the places we visit. I could hold your hand and lead you, Missie Ann?"

This time there was no mistake. His eyelids had drooped, his large Teddy Bear black eyes were pools of passion and his voice had become black velvet, as he whispered back: "I make English lady last year very, very,

very happy here for one month." My mind boggled—perhaps I was missing the chance of a lifetime! Perhaps he was secretly the great lover of all lovers. Could she really have been tucked up with him for a whole month among the rocks and the donkeys and goats, and experienced eternal bliss? Or maybe it was a yearly program for Mr. M.—part of the "service" that was expected!

I got more and more embarrassed; in fact, I think at that moment I would have preferred to be murdered—but some Celtic strength returned and I heard myself announce in my most commmanding voice: "Well, Mr. Mustapha, we must now go to bed. Remember we are watching the dawn tomorrow."

Mr. Mustapha leaped to his feet: "Oh, Missie Ann, you make me so happy. I come to you this night and we talk about film and your beautiful ideas and feelings and I help you."

"*No.*" I nearly shouted it. "*You* go back to the rest house, Mr. Mustapha, *I* sleep here. In a *tomb*," I added. And I did.

Before Mr. M. retreated back through the ravine, he murmured, "But no one is allowed to sleep here, Missie Ann, and what will you do about washing-and-etcetera?"

I answered, "I won't wash, Mr. Mustapha," and thought, "as for spending a penny I will utilize the rock rather than face a night with you." I slept on a slab—soundly and peacefully—perhaps it was my own tomb!

Next morning Mr. Mustapha and I sat gazing at the incredible sight of the dawn touching Petra like a fairy wand, transforming it into glorious pink.

We munched our bread and drank our disgusting coffee. I looked at him out of the corner of my eye. He was a Teddy Bear again. My would-be lover had vanished. Later, when we came back to make the film, he did chase me into the desert one evening and tried to make me lie down among a lot of camels and offered me a plot of his land, but the unit were there to protect me and they all got a big laugh. I had always thought of Mr. M. as being around forty years old. It turned out he was twenty-nine! What shocks one gets—but it does a girl good all the same.

It may be "See Naples and die," but it should be "See Petra and live."

> Match me such marvel
> Save in Eastern clime
> A rose-red city "half as old as time."

It is eternal, silent, beautiful and—alone.

CHAPTER 14

The Eighth Veil

Having made the film *Thunder of Silence* I returned from Jordan, and when we had finished the editing I went down to my cottage in Suffolk. I am not mentioning the name of the village as we are all rather jealous of our privacy, but I will say it is a fishing village and without doubt the most wonderful spot on earth to me. Of all the beaches I have walked on in my travels none rivals our beach—our sea—our wind—our seals— our seagulls—and best of all our skylarks. I feel anything could happen here, however strange—but then things are only called strange because we don't understand them. We may sally forth into space but now the planets are in return visiting us and their vibrations and powers are very strong.

I myself believe in spaceships and have had first-hand experience of their presence, like hundreds of people who have proof that they exist. I actually saw a spaceship over our village here five years ago and it was witnessed by others. It was six days before Christmas, there was snow on the ground and it was a beautiful clear night with the stars very close. Our village has no street lighting, so I was carrying my flashlight. There were a few Christmas trees lit up in the houses on the green and candles in the windows. Then as I turned the corner toward the pub where I was meeting some friends I saw what could have been a gigantic Christmas decoration, a kind of specimen display that one might come across in Las Vegas, advertising something or other—definitely not in keeping with our village! I turned off my light and gazed up into the sky. Then I rushed into the pub and dragged out my friends to witness what was happening—I knew it was a spaceship as I have been to many lectures on UFO's and seen drawings and films about them, but I was not prepared for the exciting sensation and awe I felt when I actually faced a real one. There it was in front of my eyes. Beings from another planet—visitors from outer space. Its silence and speed—here one moment, gone the next—seemed to offer the challenge, "Believe it or not. But we *are* here." I wonder if we are all becoming blasé or watch too many space programs on television, but our village took the whole episode in its stride as a passing event. I heard later on that spaceships have visited Suffolk once or twice before. Next time they come to us I hope very much they will land. We have plenty of space near my cottage! I will be there to greet them.

This spaceship was shaped like a large shield or kite. In the center there was what looked like a gleaming sword. The rim of the shield was surrounded by small shimmering blue lights—the brightest I have ever seen—that fluctuated in and out as if being turned on and off in rotation. From where we stood it could have been about a hundred feet above the roof of the house at the end of the village street. It hung there silently in the starlit deep blue sky. It was beautiful. We stood quite still, without speaking for about three or four minutes. My heart was thumping so hard that I thought at any moment I would "take off" and join our visitors from outer space. Suddenly the "ship" turned on its side like a streak of lightning and was gone. It was as if all its lights had been turned off by the flick of a switch and in one second it was no more. There was a strange feeling of exhilaration after its departure, no fear. Perhaps that depends on who it is in the universe that comes to look at us. When the beings from the planets do come seriously in the future, will they come in peace, want to help us? We are after all members of the same universe, and as there is supposed to be a brotherhood of man on Earth there is surely the brotherhood of the whole universe. Yet we send out dangerous vibrations into space with our atom bombs and pollution, and they may be worried that we shall become a danger to them in the future. We may be separating ourselves from beings who might be able to give us help, and wisdom far beyond that which we know on Earth, and whose laws of order in space may have succeeded better than the laws of *Homo sapiens* and for far longer. There are those who think spaceships are described at the beginning of the book of Ezekiel in the Bible, and in the New Testament as the Star from the East that led the Shepherds and the Wise Men to Bethlehem.

It interested me very much when researching for my various Diary Documentary films to read about "ships that flew in the air" millions of years ago in Atlantis, China, Mexico, etcetera. Yet it is only four hundred years ago that we firmly believed that our Earth was so important that nothing else could exist and that the sun moved around us. Whether or not we are laughed at or thought mad, shouldn't we start to acknowledge that there could surely be superior beings who might be able to guide us in the new age of Aquarius? I wish we could now demand that the governments of the world stop treating us as children or idiots, with their ridiculous explanations of what is happening and their denials of the sightings and experiences from all over the world from very reliable sources. It's no accident that the young take such a deep interest. The lectures that I go to are packed with young people, and those not so young, searching for knowledge of our universe and of our future. More and more people believe now that there is great living intelligence in the universe beyond and that we can, and do, make contact with it and it with us.

I was rather exhausted after Jordan so went straight to bed when I got home—my usual program—and stayed there for three days. Then it was out onto the beach, walking along that wild piece of coast with the east wind blowing one off one's feet, wellington boots on and a sou'wester pulled down and tied under the chin—for a talk with my Guardian Angel about where to go next—I had no idea.

I get very restless when I am not working. The pent-up frustration is often appalling, even though I try to shout it off on the beach. One day, when everything was rough and wild and there was no one in sight, I stood facing the sea with my arms above my head and shouted my commands to the universe. Then I turned around suddenly. There facing me a few feet away was an elderly man with his dog. His mouth was open and he just stared at me in amazement—so did the dog. Feeling highly embarrassed and not wanting to be shut up in some lunatic asylum, I shouted back over the wind: "Actress— sorry—so sorry—actress," as I pointed to myself—and started reciting Lady Macbeth's opening speech at a breathtaking speed.

He didn't move, nor did the dog. I felt we would be there forever, frozen into some mad picture—for people to ponder over. "What were they doing," they would say, "alone on an empty beach like that?" So I decided to break it. With a mad laugh I started to run toward my cottage. The dog was most relieved; coming to life at last, it followed me, barking furiously.

A few days later most of the plumbing in the cottage broke down and the radiators sounded like someone in the throes of a death rattle. I called our plumber—he was away. I was given the number of someone else two villages away—he said he would be around that afternoon. I opened my door to a quiet serious-looking man, I made him a cup of tea and we talked for two and a half hours. After he had gone I realized I had never shown him the radiators or the pipes. But unknown to him he had started me off on my next film.

He said, "Where are you going next, Miss Todd?"

I said, "I don't know, perhaps you can tell me?"

He answered, "Yes, I can. It's quite obvious—Scotland—Iona—the Blessed Isle in the Hebrides."

I asked him if he knew it and he said: "Yes. I went there to meditate."

I got the electric fingers down my back and realized at that moment that Iona was to be my seventh film.

I had been all over the world, but now I had to come home. So my drama on the beach *had* worked and my question had been answered. Next day the plumber left a phonograph record outside my kitchen door. It was

Mendelssohn's *Fingal's Cave*, which we later used as the theme music all through the film.

After a short holiday I returned to my flat in London and started on the synopsis for *Thunder of Light*. I then persuaded the British Tourist Board to send me to Iona and give me the money to make the film.

The journey by train to this island in the Hebrides takes longer than flying to Nepal. One takes the night sleeper to Crianlarick for breakfast, then on to Oban, Argyllshire, then the steamer sailing through the Western Isles with their mists and mystery. There is a saying in the Highlands that "God made the Western Isles and covered it all with mist because it was so beautiful. He was afraid that if He could see it He would want to take it back again."

After the Isles, there is a bus ride of two hours across the Island of Mull, then the wait for the ferry *and* the weather to cross the water to Iona.

Iona is only three and a half miles long and one and a quarter miles wide but in this little isle a lamp was lit whose flame lighted pagan Europe. St. Columba landed here in A.D. 563 with twelve of his companion monks from Ireland and brought Christianity to a dark world.

People come from all over the globe to this "Blessed Isle," which consists of only rock and heather but is associated always with things of the spirit. There is nowhere to stay—except one very small hotel on the quayside—and when the great storms are raging one is cut off completely from Mull and the mainland by twenty-foot waves.

The island is dominated by the Abbey of St. Columba, the monk, prince, priest, healer, saint and friend of the people. What I loved and found very moving was the tiny healing chapel of the saint, so small that one had to bend to get inside. Above the altar are pinned the names of the local sick, asking for prayers of healing. It was completely peaceful with the snow-white doves circling above.

There is a well-known legend about St. Columba. It says that one day he sent one of his monks from the monastery down to the shore to receive a bird that he had "seen in the spirit" with a broken wing flying in a storm from Ireland. The bird later arrived and the monk stayed with it while it rested for three days. The saint gave it absent healing and then it recovered and flew away.

The pilgrims who come here are mostly young people. There was only one car on the island, so I bicycled in my kilt and made many friends, because I was a Scot. I was immensely happy.

The Hill of Dun-I is the only large hill on the island and when you get to the top you look over two thousand miles of the Atlantic Ocean straight to Labrador. It is strange and Celtic. When we were filming one scene there in a tremendous gale and rain, the camera had to be tied down, and Tom Taylor, the director, shouted down to me, as I was literally crawling up the rocks below, my head covered with a raincoat, and very frightened. "Stay where you are, Ann. You won't be able to stand up here. We will have one more try but may have to give up."

It all seemed very far from Hollywood. I crouched under a boulder while the wind and rain lashed up into a fury that seemed to be attacking me as if with arrows. I got into such a ridiculous state of fright that I thought anything was better than being alone, and so I started again to try to climb up and join them. But I was unlucky and fell into a deep cleft in the rock and immediately suffered quite bad pain in my leg and thigh. Tom arranged to have me carried down the hill, and I was put to bed. The nearest doctor was five hours away by boat and anyway only came if you were dying, and no one had pain-killing drugs. Later someone went over to Mull, and then on to Oban and obtained some pills.

I was lying on my side—I couldn't move and the pain had now become really bad. I was desperately worried, because this was holding up the filming. Then one of the unit told me that he had heard there was a convention for "healers" from all over the world on the island and asked if I would like to see one of them. I agreed at once. The door of my bedroom opened and in he came, but I couldn't turn around. He came over to the bed, knelt down and passed his hands over me without touching and said a prayer, very quietly.

I felt nothing—but at last when he had finished I struggled around to look at him, out of politeness, and to thank him. He had one of the kindest faces I have ever seen in my life. His eyes showed great concern.

He said, "Please, are you better?"

I lied. "Yes, much better."

"I am so happy," he said, "because you see, it is very important to me—you are my first."

But the pain definitely did become better and I was able to get downstairs, with help. I bowed to my healer— he reciprocated with a big smile. I felt suddenly that maybe I had got it all wrong, that I wasn't in Iona to make a film at all but just to give this man encouragement to continue in hope and certainty with his healing. The unit teased me of course. The laugh was on them in the end as, when we eventually finished the film and got home, I saw my doctor. He said I had put my pelvis out quite badly and, as hardly ever happens, it had gone back of its own accord. I wish I had been able to send a telegram of congratulations to my healer.

My story of *Thunder of Light* is about two women in

need of help. I play the parts of both women. It is said
that "you don't go to Iona, Iona calls for *you*." The first
lady is called for and is followed by the other character, a
mysterious figure in deep mourning, with a black veil
completely hiding her face. As the film progresses you
realize the "Lady in Black" is seeking help in her terrible
grief at the death of someone she loved. The island
comforts her and teaches her that her sorrow can only be
distressing to her loved one, who is close to her and
happy. When she returns to her cottage, although there
is no one there, the room is full of music, laughter and
light and there is a feeling of love and welcome.

At the end of the film there is a shot of me sitting on
the very top of the hill Dun-I. Then in slow motion I
dissolve into the Lady in Black. The wind is blowing her
veil as if trying to tear it off. Over this, music plays and I
recite the Yeats lines:

> The wind blows out of the gates of the day
> The wind blows over the lonely of heart
> And the lonely of heart is withered away.

She then takes off her black hat, black veil and her black
gloves and, for the first time one sees that the two women
are really one—and I have also got my answer to the call
of Iona.

Of all the films I have made to date, this is the most
rewarding. David Lean once said to me, "Every film
should be made, small or big, on at least three levels," and
I try to make each of mine like this. Firstly, it must be
beautiful to look at, with lovely and evocative music, and,
most important, a theme tune that links the film all the
way through. Secondly, there must be instant knowledge
of the country I am visiting, and, thirdly, a deeper

dimension of meaning that one hopes will move people.

Thunder of Light is a real challenge to an audience and I am absolutely thrilled with the letters I get from people who have liked it and have understood its full meaning and been inspired by it.

I have met many people since who have also heard this call from Iona and have experienced what I did, and now the island is becoming a kind of club for young and old. Here is a radiating energy, a place of pilgrimage for individuals trying to get together. Here one is recharged. This tiny island, so strong with its secret spell, has had the power to draw and hold men of many lands and needs, throughout the centuries.

I would like to finish by quoting what I said at the end of the film because it sums up Iona to me. "This mystic isle—here the wind and the waves hear the messages from the unknown beyond."

It was in Iona that, for me, a veil was lifted.

CHAPTER 15

"I Painted Peace"

Thunder of Light made in Scotland is the seventh film in my series. Seven is my very lucky number—so maybe this should be the last of my films, and I will now change gears again and start another phase of my life—as long as I don't go into reverse!

Meanwhile, I went to Moscow in 1977 and Israel in 1978 as their guest to discuss two more possible films to add to the series. Moscow was fantastic. Red Square with the snow falling on the Kremlin and the beautiful gold turnip-shaped tops to the buildings was everything one had dreamed about.

I was taken for a Russian woman several times on the Metro. My handsome Cossack guide said, "Oh, yes, with your high cheekbones and with your scarf on, you *are* Russian, but when you take it off, you are not—your hair is *so* straight." Russian ladies were wearing their hair piled up on their heads and lots of curls—a bit like usherettes in the past in cinemas. I think they must have thought I hadn't bothered with mine, as the *directrice* of the film studio tried very hard to make an appointment for me to have it curled at the hairdresser.

Their Metros have been written about so much, but they really are glamorous with their marble mosaics and busts of Pushkin and their famous poets. It might cheer things up to look at Shakespeare and Byron when traveling from High Street, Kensington, to Barons Court! The trains are an attractive blue-green color and travel at a great speed, and everything is spotlessly clean and shining white.

I went to their famous Circus and Puppet Show and attended one of their mass weddings of six couples—the brides all dressed in white, which surprised me. Afterward as is the tradition they all went in the blinding snow to lay their bouquets on the war memorial at the foot of the Kremlin wall, and to give thanks to those who had died for them in the war.

My meeting with the gentleman from the Politburo, to discuss the film and my synopsis for it, was interesting but a bit frightening.

I had come alone to Moscow and had only mixed with Russians. Each morning I sat on my bed at the Hotel Rosia, facing the Kremlin—waiting—hoping someone would collect me. I had no rubles and had come over, rather grandly, without a visa (I had met the Gromykos which helped). The British Embassy had suggested very kindly that I stay with them—maybe they thought I might be whisked away as a pawn. But as it was so important to have the Russians' trust, I did not accept and avoided everything British till my last night, when I did accept the ambassador's invitation to dinner.

At the meeting to discuss the film I sat on one side of the table, alone except for the interpreter who had to sit behind me, and faced them all. Opposite me was a short heavy man with tiny eyes. On either side of him sat three obviously inferior gentlemen, who seemed nervous, and at either end of the long table sat a large lady with a notebook and pencil.

No one smiled. The chief gentleman, whom I will call Mr. S., was so close to me across the narrow table that divided us that we could have held hands. A flowery speech of welcome was made to me, translated into English, about how honored they were to have me, especially as I was a Shakespearean actress. (To my relief it was not, for once, *The Seventh Veil!*) They didn't look it. Then three sharp questions were asked by Mr. S., and the "interrogation" began. One, what did it mean in my script by "the shooting will begin . . ."? They didn't care for that. Two, what did it mean in the agreement "the film will be made according to usual contracts and carried out, the exceptions being an Act of God—fire—or war, et-cetera"? He liked that even less. *"What war?" "Aren't we friends?"* he said, and however much I kept saying, "Oh, don't take any notice of that Mr. S., that doesn't mean a thing, it is in all film contracts, no one takes any notice of *that*," he *did*, and went on and on about it.

Then to my horror he snapped at me: "I wish to talk money."

"Oh, *I* never do that—that's the producer's job back home."

"Then why are you here as our guest, paid for by us?"

"But how terrible—there has been a serious misunder-standing. Oh, I feel so embarrassed." I picked my bag up off the floor—sometimes I am not an actress for nothing—and rose to my feet. "Please put me on your

Aeroflot plane this afternoon and I will go home. I am so sorry if it is my fault." Mr. S. signed to me to sit down. I smiled at him and thought "now is my moment," so— leaning forward, our noses nearly touching—I said, "I will talk about the artistic side, Mr. S.," and I launched forth with my ideas.

I told him that someone at home who knew about these things had suggested that we could use one of their old war planes and put our cameras where the guns used to be, slow down the film so that on screen it goes faster, then fly only two hundred feet above the ground right across Russia—from the Urals to the Black Sea. Because of the speed the land would look like some psychedelic painting. Over this, Rimsky-Korsakoff would be played very loud, then the scene would cut to a small flower in Suzdal, the village which is part of the Golden Ring around Moscow. I explained that as the film ran only half an hour it would be impossible to show the immensity of their land, but done this way it would make a tremendous opening impact on the audience. No one spoke, so I continued gaining confidence. "I would like to recite the poem 'Snow' by your famous poet Yevtushenko, if it were possible. I want to film one scene in Siberia—from a sledge—and over the poem, two young people would act the story like a ballet in the snow. Could you let me go to Siberia now—as I am here—and film this scene with a Russian cameraman, do you think?" I paused for breath.

Mr. S.'s face suddenly broke into a terrifying smile and he said, "Madame, if and when we allow this film to be made, we will bring the snow to you."

I then bought (on my company) a near-white fur coat to blend in with Siberia and sat waiting in my flat in London for the summons.

Much correspondence, all in Russian, has gone backward and forward. My neighbor speaks Russian and has lived there in the past, and she is quite used to letters being pushed under her door at all hours by me, to be translated immediately. But, though I received a telegram after my departure from Russia saying, "We love you," I am afraid this is the only time I have failed—so far.

But one never knows—the fur coat and I are still waiting.

I am also very much hoping to carry out my plan to make a film in Israel. I cannot remember why I first went there, except that I have always longed to walk over the land where Abraham and Christ walked—and I have admired so much the courage of the people. Unless one has been there, one can have no idea of their vulnerability; it is a David and Goliath story.

The government arranged for a sensitive and perceptive Jew to interpret for and look after me during my visit. I could have fallen in love with him—and he with me! Perhaps it is ridiculous, but I hope I continue all my life to be in love with someone or something. It gives such color and joy to everything.

I think I wrote one of my best synopses for Israel, and I hope and pray one day when things are calmer we will make this film.

It was an unforgettable experience—walking in the desert where Abraham walked—standing where the Christ stood. In the little Church of the Loaves and Fishes at Galilee, my Jewish friend read the story to me out of the Bible. Walking up the hill of the Sermon on the Mount, the roses of Sharon still growing under our feet—sitting by the Lake of Galilee, "seeing" Christ in the fishing boats, and feeling so strongly that Jesus was beside me, I seemed to hear, like an echo over the water,

"Follow me." Then the agony of the Via Dolorosa—the Stations of the Cross—the Mountain of Temptation outside Jericho—a high mountain with a monastery on top where Jesus was tempted for the forty days and forty nights. Then, eating enormous oranges picked straight from the trees.

My friend took me to dinner one night at a smart restaurant facing the Tower of David. We ate off gold plates and afterward we strolled through Old Jerusalem, lit up like a golden city at 3 A.M. When we reached the Wailing Wall there were a few businessmen worshipping there before going to their offices and, on the other side of the partition, a dozen women. I asked him if I could join them. He said, "Of course."

I put my shawl over my head and went to the women's side of the wall. Without knowing it, I put my arms in the correct position and pressed my face against it. I stayed there over ten minutes. When I returned to my friend and guide I was crying.

He looked at me and said, "As a Jew I don't believe in such things, but I think at some time you have been here before." I had—I knew.

In the sun we sat outside the Damascus Gate eating their tiny hard-boiled eggs with the round bread with a hole in the middle, and watching the world go by.

At night Jerusalem is a golden city of magic. In the dawn, as it wakes up, you first hear the twittering of their strange little birds, then the Muslim call to prayer, then the ringing bells of the Catholic and Protestant churches, all mingling together into one great call of joy to God.

I found this very touching poem in Jerusalem, written by an Arab child, aged thirteen and a half:

*   *   *

The Paint Box

I had a paint box,
Each color glowing with delight.
I had a paint box with colors
Warm and cool and bright.

I had no red for wounds and blood,
I had no black for an orphaned child,
I had no white for the face of the dead,
I had no yellow for burning sands.

I had orange for joy and life,
I had green for birds and blooms,
I had blue for clean, bright skies,
I had pink for dreams and rest.

   I sat down
      and painted Peace.

Shalom

CHAPTER 16

Before the Dawn

"Faith is a bird that *feels* the light and sings
when it is dark before the dawn."

Tagore

Now, for the moment, I am back in my cottage in Suffolk by the sea. This part of the world is full of the atmosphere of history. Constable came from around here and so did Gainsborough. Wagner was nearly shipwrecked off these coasts while escaping from his creditors, but he was compensated for the discomforts of the hazardous voyage by getting the idea for his opera *The Flying Dutchman*.

You have to be tough and have resilience to face the flat Suffolk coastlands, east winds and sometimes frightening seas that decide to attack without warning. If you want lush golden sands, like parts of Cornwall, or picture-postcard blue sea, or smooth rolling hills, don't come here. Here you will find pebbles, marshes, flood tides, force-ten gales and what one of our fishermen calls a "changing live" beach. Then out of the grayness and elemental forces there is suddenly color—wallflowers, skylarks—and *magic;* and always neighbors on the village green inquiring if you are all right because they haven't seen you around for a few days. A present of shrimps from a fisherman on his way home is found tied outside the kitchen door—and when the electricity fails because a swan has flown into a cable, we are much more concerned with the swan and its recovery than with having no telephone or light.

The seen and unseen are very close here. When I am on the beach I sometimes feel that I float into another world. A few years ago I experienced a wonderful moment while walking barefoot along the shore. I only wish Jung or perhaps Blake had been able to give us a new name for such moments. I suppose it is like finding oneself in another dimension and seeing, hearing and feeling certain things that don't get into the known even though one has "known" them deep down before.

I was standing on the edge of the sea, standing so still I was hardly breathing, when a strange mist enveloped me. The sun disappeared. Then it seemed I was stretching out my arm and, like Alice in Wonderland, I felt as though it was getting longer and longer until it reached far out to sea. I then opened my hand and collected a handful of water and drew my arm slowly back to the shore. I heard far away, in my head as an echo: "Religion should be like a vast moving ocean—the Sea of Spirituality. Why do you dip your hand in it and take out creeds, which then become static, fixed, and never-changing? Spirituality is always moving like the universe. Dip your hand in again and remember: 'The spirit of God *moved* on the face of the waters.'"

I then—what can one call it?—woke up; and the sea

was sea—the sand was sand—the seagull looking at me a seagull; and I was me again. The sun was out.

Here, if one wishes to believe, one can be a channel for Higher Powers. I have always found I can get guidance especially over my work, but of course the responsibility for decision is ultimately my own. I realized some years ago that I couldn't live any longer without searching for the answer to many things. Now I am beginning to realize that the only reality is in the World of Spirit and is reflected by those in that world back to us. I feel they are there waiting for our recognition and our desire for help, and then it will be given, as it always has been. Now, we are beginning to lose faith and think that we can "go it alone." Perhaps we can't; but, if we have the courage to acknowledge this, then with their love:

A thousand unseen hands reach down to help you
    to their peace-crowned heights,
And all the forces of the firmament shall fortify your
    strength.
    Be not afraid.